SCIPIO STORYTELLING

Talk in a Southern Indiana Community

Margaret Read MacDonald

University Press of America, Inc.
Lanham • New York • London

Copyright © 1996 by
University Press of America,® Inc.
4720 Boston Way
Lanham, Maryland 20706

3 Henrietta Street
London, WC2E 8LU England

Library of Congress Cataloging-in-Publication Data

MacDonald, Margaret Read.
Scipio storytelling : talk in a southern Indiana community / Margaret
Read MacDonald.
p.   cm.
Includes index.
1. Folklore--Indiana--Scipio (Jennings County) 2. Storytelling--
Indiana--Scipio (Jennings County). 3. Scipio (Jennings County,
Ind.)--Social life and customs. I. Title.
GR110.I6M33   1996   398'.09772'17--dc20   96-15649 CIP

ISBN 0-7618-0349-1 (cloth: alk. ppr.)
ISBN 0-7618-0350-5 (pbk: alk. ppr.)

This Book is Dedicated to

Spiv and Esther
and
Sally and Pert

And to all the good folks

at Scipio, Indiana.

ACKNOWLEDGMENTS

*   *   *

Thanks to Sally Read Johnston for proofreading this manuscript, to Julie MacDonald for typing it, and to Nat Whitman for the formatting. Thanks also to Barre Toelken, John H. McDowell, and Judy O'Malley for critiquing the work.

*   *   *

Thanks to Pat Zohrlaut for putting me up and putting up with me on those many visits to Scipio. And my heartfelt thanks to all the Scipio folks who fed me and encouraged me in this long, long project. Thanks especially to the church ladies of the Scipio Presbyterian Church for making both this book and my Scipio history *Threads from the Past* available for purchase in Scipio.

*   *   *

CONTENTS

PREFACE

This is a journey into private space... the world of a small rural community in Southern Indiana. I thank the talkers in this book for letting me put them on tape. They didn't expect to be analyzed quite so strenuously. But I hope they will enjoy my comments and approve.

As a professional storyteller and a teacher of fledgling storytellers, I spend much of my time watching other tellers, trying to figure out why their stories work...or don't work. And wondering why my own stories work...when they do. My strong point as a teller seems to be that the rhythms of storytelling come naturally to me. I expect they come so naturally because I spent my childhood listening. Listening to talkers who shaped their stories so skillfully that a roomful of youngsters and oldsters could sit upright on straight-backed chairs all night and just listen, glad to be there.

But why were these talkers so fascinating? Their talk clearly knew nothing of grammar or elocution manuals. But unwritten rules and strictly-defined levels of skill were there.

So I went home to listen again. And this time I taped the conversations, over 200 hours worth. Then I transcribed them and listened again. And after I had read everything I could find that other listeners had written about the storyteller's art, I decided what *I* thought. And here it is.

Let's begin with a visit to two New Year's Eve parties in Scipio. First we will just sit and listen while folks talk, and then I will have a bit to say about the storytelling you have witnessed. To relate my comments to theories on these subjects by other scholars see the tale notes at each chapter's end.

If you have your own agenda for using this book feel free to skip around and read just the "good parts" as you define them.

In the book's second half, I investigate the style of one Scipio teller, Spiv Helt, Scipio's acknowledged master teller.

Let me start by introducing Scipio and her talkers.

SCIPIO:

Southern Indiana. A small rural community. *Very* small. A corner grocery (formerly a general store), a take-out pizza place (formerly a bank), two churches, a grade school (formerly K-12), a garage (gas no longer available), and a tiny post office. Fifty or so houses. Rich farm land stretching away down the Sand Creek river bottom in one direction. Hilly, wooded, gullied, not so rich land stretching off in the other.

THE SCIPIO TALKERS:

Gordon "Spiv" Helt: Acknowledged as one of Scipio's best storytellers. In his 80's at the time these stories were transcribed. Grew up as a poor farm boy on Sand Creek. Dropped out of Scipio High School pretty quick, but not before falling in love with Esther Green. Married her as soon as she finished teacher's training. Sold tobacco for the A.J. Reynolds Company for a while, then settled down to farming. Now owns acres of rich bottom land on Sand Creek. Built a fine brick home on a hill overlooking Scipio. Drove a school bus for years, is a pillar of the community, and served as County Road Commissioner for a while. Called "Spiv" because as a country boy from Rock Creek School, he didn't know anybody at Scipio High so just called them all after a cartoon character "Spivens.""They turned it on me," he says.

Esther Helt: Spiv's wife. A grade school teacher in Scipio for years. A pillar of the Scipio Presbyterian Church. No children, but Aunt Esther to numerous Helt family nieces and nephews in the area. A fantastic cook. Straight backed, straight-laced, but with a twinkling eye. The perfect foil for Spiv's storying.

Paul "Pert" Helt: Spiv's younger brother. Quiet, bemused, easy to laugh. Tells stories only when Spiv defers to him.Also farmed rich Sand Creek bottom land. His son, Gerald, now farms all of his land plus Spiv's, plus numerous leased tracts. "Pert" because he was so "purty" in high school.

Sally Helt: Pert's wife. Petite, pretty, kind. A great sense of humor and a good conversationalist. Also a fantastic cook. Sings in the Presbyterian Church choir, active in the Home Demonstration Club, raised two sons and looked after five grandkids. The sons live on property adjoining Pert and Sally's farm.

Jack McConnell: Son of Frank McConnell, Spiv's good friend, who ran the general store for years. Jack, in his sixties, works as auditor for the State and commutes to Indianapolis (120 miles round trip). Another pillar of the community and the Presbyterian Church, Jack lives with wife Ledell in a small 1950's subdivision just north of Scipio. Jack's storytelling ability comes naturally from a childhood spent in listening at McConnell's Store.

Wally Hines: Made a good career at Cummins Engine Company in nearby Columbus, Indiana. Recently retired, Wally lives with wife Marybelle in a handsome brick home atop a hill just down a country road out of Scipio. Wally is active in the Presbyterian Church, and Volunteer Fire Department. Marybelle is an organist for the church.

Nolan Spencer: The trickster, teaser, "bad boy" of the bunch. Went to school with Jack and Wally. I get the feeling Nolan would be a lot more fun in a men-only telling than in mixed company. Lives with his wife Margaret just out of Scipio. Margaret works in the Post Office. Nolan works at Cummins.

Because of the format of my taping, consisting of interviews with Spiv and Esther and mixed-group living room conversations, these are the tellers who emerged and will be discussed here. Other folks who appear on tape might well be talkers in their own right in different settings. Some of the women, such as Marybelle Hines, are remarkable storytellers but I didn't get them on tape. Nor are all *men* storytellers in the "living room conversation" format which I taped. Bill Byford, host for a New Year's Eve party, spoke hardly a word during the entire evening.

My mother, herself a Scipio farm girl, went to school with Spiv, Pert, and Esther Helt. Spiv and Esther were my parents' closest friends and many childhood evenings were spent at their house. Esther and my mother were cousins too, and anyway, Scipio ties run strong. So I am sort of family to the Helts.

THE TAPING

I visited Scipio twice a year fairly regularly between July 1978 and October 1985, stopping off for a week each time, en route to East Coast conferences. The community knew I was collecting "Spiv's Stories" and local history. My technique was taped participant conversation. I just turned on the tape recorder and let it run...all day, every day. I have transcribed over 100 hours of the 200+ hours collected, selecting those in which the most storytelling took place.

PART I
SCIPIO STORIES

The telling of stories is considered an art in Scipio, Indiana. "Spiv's quite a storyteller," folks say. Or "That Jack can really tell them!" High praise. Everyone likes to hear a good story.

The men tell stories at the garage, at the Scipio store, at the barbershop. Women tell stories at the beauty shop, over refreshments at the Ladies Aid meetings. And when folks get together for an evening's visit the stories usually come out. A "story" in Scipio is a structured, humorous anecdote about something that happened to someone in Scipio or someone known to someone who lives in Scipio. Travelling jokes are also told but seem less important to most Scipio tellers than stories that "really happened."

Not every evening of talk will bring forth "stories" but folks feel a sense of accomplishment and delight with those evenings which do produce a string of good stories. "You should have been out at Pert's last night. Spiv really got going!" If you can get a good teller started, the evening's entertainment is assured.

This all may seem quite casual and artless, but indeed there is a great deal of artistry involved in this conversational storytelling. The rules of the game for both audience and teller are definite, clearly understood by everyone in this southern Indiana rural culture. Both teller and audience perform their roles so smoothly that the artistry of the event goes unnoticed, though its aesthetic impact is felt. Let's spend a couple of evenings with some Scipio folks and listen to them talk. Then we'll take a closer look at just what is going on when Scipio folks "get to telling stories."

CHAPTER 1
NEW YEAR'S EVE 1984

Every New Year's Eve Spiv and Esther Helt get together with a group of close friends for a big party. No one knows just how long the group's New Year's Eve parties have been going on, but everyone thinks it must have been at least twenty years now. They take turns having the whole group over. The hostess prepares the entire meal, usually quite a feast. Lately there has been clamor among some of the women to make this event a potluck and thus take the burden off one person. But in the New Year's Eve of 1984, one woman still prepared the whole meal. The members of the New Year's Eve group are: Spiv and Esther Helt; Spiv's sister Margueritte Byford and her husband, Bill Byford; Spiv's brother Paul "Pert" Helt and wife Sally; Jack and Ledell McConnell; Wally and Marybelle Hines; Nolan and Margaret Spencer. Throughout this evening younger people drifted in and out. The Byford's grandson and wife had helped prepare the meal but left to go to their own party. Grandson Jeff stayed until time to go to work at 10 p.m. up at Columbus. Wally's daughter Laura arrived around 10:30 P.M. and Wally's son

Scott came in after he finished work at Amick's restaurant down in North Vernon. My nine year old daughter, Julie, and I were visiting Spiv and Esther, and were also guests this evening.

Despite their age differences, the ties in this group are many. All are members of the Presbyterian Church in Scipio. Marybelle plays the piano and Wally, Jack, Ledell and Nolan sing in the choir. The women all belong to the Ladies Aid and everyone in this group tries to make it to the monthly church Birthday Breakfast at Amick's Restaurant in North Vernon whenever possible.

Jack McConnell's father, Frank, was one of Spiv's close buddies when he was living. Wally is an old fishing buddy of Spiv's. Wally, Nolan, and Bill Byford all have worked up at Cummins. Nolan and Spiv have both driven the school bus. All of the men have been part of the Scipio Volunteer Fire Department. And Esther taught Jack, Wally, and Nolan when they were in grade school up at Scipio.

NEW YEAR'S EVE AT THE BYFORD'S
DECEMBER 31, 1983

The sidewalk to the back door has been salted to let us in. We climb two steps and enter through the back porch, into the kitchen. Margueritte greets us warmly. The kitchen table, loaded with food, is laid out to one side. Grandsons Wes and Jeff and Wes' wife are working at the kitchen sink and refrigerator putting the final touches on. Right away Wes and wife leave for their own party. They have worked all day getting this spread ready. Margueritte says grandson Jeff always comes over to help her cook; he loves to cook and is good at it.

The other guests arrive in quick succession. Boisterous Jack McConnell and a smiling Ledell clamor in; tall, red-haired Wally Hines and talkative Marybelle are parking their car in the snow and hurrying in behind. Nolan and Margaret Spencer, who live just across the road, put on their boots and come on over as soon as they see the guests arriving.

We go into the living room...very small as is usual in this era house...couch, coffee table, three easy chairs and a wooden rocker...card table set up in the middle with four chairs...pine tree lit, covered with homemade ornaments. Large wooden-cabineted TV in one corner. Fudge and peanut butter candy set out on trays on the coffee table...bowls of unsalted pretzels, and peanuts too.

We are ready to eat at six. Everyone gets nervous about 6:15 because Pert and Sally haven't come yet. Margueritte thinks they would have called if they weren't coming. There is no mention of calling them to ask. It is long distance because of the way the phone districts are set up.

At six-thirty we begin to eat regardless. Some say that Pert and Sally would be here by now if they were coming. Everyone assembles in the kitchen in a semi-circle eyeballing the laden table. Margueritte asks everyone to "Come on." The stragglers in the living room stop gabbing and come stand in the kitchen door. Margueritte announces that Wally is going to say grace. Wally, standing tall and impressively devout, blesses both us for the coming year and the food, without driving us yet to foot-shifting or stages of drool. The group relaxes and shuffles self-consciously not wanting to seem too eager to be first while Margueritte announces "DIG IN." Nine year old Julie leaves my side and races for the pile of paper plates at the table's end. I gasp "Julie!" and she retreats, mortified at having committed a social blunder, to hide her head in her mother's skirts. Wally and a couple of others start picking up plates and Julie tentatively joins the beginning of a line. Everyone falls in and paper plates are piled with thinly sliced cheeses, three kinds of sandwich meats (beef, turkey, ham), three kinds of breads, mustards, plenty of deviled eggs, two kinds of molded jello-and-fruit salads (green with canned pear halves, red with fruit cocktail), potato chips, and a flat casserole of baked beans hot from the oven all brown-sugary and delicious. There is a huge container of red punch and ice to ladle into Styrofoam cups.

We carry our loaded plates to card tables covered with pretty paper Christmas tablecloths and Christmas napkins. Eight can be seated at the two card tables, one in the kitchen, one in the living room. TV trays appear from somewhere and others cluster around joining the card-table group in the kitchen. There is no shortage of straight chairs. The living room fills with eaters sitting on the couch and in easy chairs, making a large circle around the four card table eaters in the room's center.

The kitchen holds all the women except Ledell and Spiv. The living room drew all the men except Spiv, and Ledell at the card table. Margueritte wanders back and forth worrying that all is alright.

The conversation keeps up a pretty good pace while the pack munches away. Reports are made on the latest illnesses of the group and their acquaintances. Margueritte's furnace broke on Christmas Eve just as her guests were leaving. Bill called the furnace man from Columbus and he came right down. They didn't get to bed until 2 A.M. Margaret Spencer's fireplace is cracked and workmen must come soon to take out the whole thing...a huge floor to ceiling Indiana limestone edifice with openings into both family and living room. Margaret dreads having the workmen come and can't visualize how they can rearrange the furniture after the remodeling. She is comforted by the realization that all this will mean replacing the old carpet! She thinks her husband Nolan hasn't figured that out yet.

Just about the time we all begin to rise for seconds, Pert and Sally arrive. Wally and Jack go out to help get Sally in. She needs to be just about carried part of the way because of her injured leg. She appears at the doorway in a walker looking rosy and full of cheer, hobbles into the kitchen to direct the filling of her plate and sits at the card table to join us.

After we all finish our seconds, we dump our plates in the garbage and shuffle a bit. Ledell comes in to join the women in the kitchen and Spiv moves to the living room where he takes possession of a big easy chair. Bill Byford, host, sits all evening in what must be HIS chair. Wally and Jack take the card table, Nolan Spencer takes the last easy chair and thus spread over half the room which is not couch, they begin to exchange tales. I sense the moment and hurry in with my tape recorder to join them.

Wally, Jack, and Nolan were in high school together. Wally says, "Since we've finished eating, I can tell this" and tells of rescuing old Mrs. Siemier who burned to death in her bed. The boys from the high school had been called to fight the fire. Wally's rather gruesome tale tells of lowering her from the second story in a bed sheet. She died later.

They go on to other topics and warm to their tale telling. Marybelle comes in from the kitchen. "I didn't want to miss this." She sits beside me on the couch and the storytelling continues. Soon all of the women have drifted in and everyone is tightly packed into one small room.

"Why are they all coming into one room?" Julie asks her mother. No one answers. It is 8:30 P.M.

Nolan tells 9-year-old Julie that Esther used to be his second grade teacher. Jack and Wally chime in...Esther taught them too. Jack begins to tell old school tales. Jack tells of breaking out the schoolhouse window, of playing checkers with the janitors in the furnace room, of playing hooky to go to a baseball game with the team on the principal's *orders*.

Jack: I tell you though
the darndest thing I ever had happen.
And I was innocent to this.
But the maddest I ever seen a teacher...was Helen Jolly.
And Glen was principal.
And I went home from school for dinner.
And when I came back from lunch from Scipio...
They were loadin' the bus out there...
And of course then they played softball, see,
and they loaded up about noon...
and they'd go and get back before school was out.
Well I was a fifth grader and the high school was gettin'
**   in the bus.**
And Glen Milholland was right there at the door.
And Glen, you know, he was always pullin' somethin'.
And he said..."You wanta go to the ball game, Jack?"
And I said "Yeah!"
And I put my...now this is the truth.
I put my foot on the first step...
and I started to get out and run towards the building...
And he said, "Where are you going?"
I said, "I'm goin' to tell my teacher."

He said, "Oh you don't have to do that. She won't miss
    you anyway."
And he said, "We're in a hurry anyway. Get in here."
I came back in the bus and went to that ball game.
Well, if the principal tells you to do that, you think
you're all right.
And so then...ten minutes before school was out...
Course we pulled in...you know.
And naturally nothin' to do but...
I should have really just went home.
But instead...well that was a BIG DEAL...
So I just walked on up into Helen's room...you know.
And she said, "Where you been."
I said, "I've been to the ball game."
"Well who gave you permission to go to the ball game?"
I said, "Mr. Milholland."
And she specifically said, "Why didn't you come and
tell me?"
I said, "I wanted to come and tell you but Mr.
    Milholland said we didn't have time and get in that
    bus...that you wouldn't miss me anyway."
Man she slammed that old door!
And she headed for the office.
I know her and Glen had a pretty good go around.
She come back and apologized to me.
Said, "Well. I think Mr. Milholland was wrong."
Said, "I don't blame YOU."
That was a mad woman.
But that's old Glen up and down.
He'd DO that.

A woman agrees, "Yeah, that's Glen all right."
Everyone mutters agreement, chuckling at Glen's easy-

going nature as a principal. The conversation turns reluctantly to Glen's present condition. He and his wife live in a small house right on the highway in the middle of Scipio. Glen's physical and mental condition aren't too good anymore though. Someone who hasn't heard the latest news about Glen asks innocently, "Does Glen get out much anymore?" Everyone chuckles nervously at this question. Spiv finally provides the logically humorous answer which the group would rather not face. "Well...he gets out when they don't *want* him to." Glen had been found wandering up and down the middle of the highway at four A.M. a few nights ago. Fortunately someone discovered him and got him back into bed before he got hit by a car.

The conversation turns to local gossip. A friend is recovering from open-heart surgery; an eighteen-year-old boy they know of has been taken to the mental hospital at Madison; an acquaintance of Jack's was thrown on a water ride in Disney World and broke three ribs. This leads into a discussion of insurance agents. And Jack suddenly gets onto house building and takes the floor.

Jack: I've decided.
If I ever build another house.
If I could go back and forth in years now...and then
build one...
I'm gonna build one with zippered walls.

Suddenly the women are all laughing at Jack's story. They were ostensibly engaged in other conversations at the time Jack started talking, but must have been listening with one ear. Sounds like they have heard this recitation before.

Jack: And the fireplace would be on castors.

You know that, Spiv?

Jack captures Spiv's attention and the room quiets except for a bit of woman's teasing still going on.

Jack: I've learned.
In forty years...I've learned.
If I ever build a new house...
The walls will have zippers in them. See?
You just zip them out and move them out...
And then the fireplace...I'll just put her on castors.
And when she...wants to make a bedroom out of that
    one...and a family room...
That fireplace...just roll her right over there!

Marybelle: Build us TWO like that, Jack. And we'll buy
    one of 'em.
Esther: Build THREE. We will too.

Everyone is laughing and gabbling about Jack's novel idea.

Spiv: It'd be easier to get a different WOMAN.

Jack's far-fetched notion is necessitated only by the wife's incessant urge to rearrange.

Esther: (setting Jack up for another story) I don't know
    about a ZIPPER or not.

Jack: (taking the bait) The reason I want...

Folks are still talking among each other and not fixating on Jack so he pauses and tries again for control of the room. He is going to tell a story.

Jack: The reason I wanted it ZIPPERED.
Cause I can handle THEM.
Now that I've got proof for that.
Esther: Awww can he HANDLE a zipper.
Jack: Now I've got PROOF of THAT.
I can take care of them zippers.

Everyone begins to gabble about the coming story...which everyone has heard except myself.

Marybelle: You want that story on TAPE, Jack?
Wally: I believe that was as mad as I've ever SEEN
**   Jackie.**

Jack: I'll tell you what I've got...Margaret.
We had a new suitcase.

The gabbling begins to die down. Here comes the story.

Jack: She got it with...top value stamps...
We took a trip and we went to COVINGTON.
We was going to the ball game...
Well first we was going to Cincinnati to the ball game.
And you couldn't buy...
You couldn't BUY, BEG, BORRY, or STEAL a room in
**   Cincinnati to stay so we went over to Covington...**
And we got a room...
And this new suitcase...

**One of these that zipped on the outside you know clear
   around
Well it was BRAND new.
We got ready to get it one morning...er zip that sucker...**

The tape ends here and has to be flipped over. Jack pauses
in his tale; then goes right on.

**So we got ready to open that up...
And it got caught.
And I worked on it you know.**

The women are adding in comments, teasing Jack.

**I stayed cool.
Didn't want to get MAAD...or nothin' like that.
People around there, you know.
Well the longer I worked...
I got a little bit...UN-tolerant.**

The women's teasing rises in level; they are chuckling.

**Esther: Here it comes...
Wally: The redder his FACE got...
Ledell: His FACE got red...
Jack: Finally when I give that one yank on it there, well
   it come loose.
We just...
Shredded that zipper all the way around it there...
   Tore her out of there and we just laid her back and
   you could...
Could get all the clothes you wanted.**

The end of Jack's line is almost lost amid the audience's laughter.
Spiv is muttering about bailin' wire needed.

Jack: Well IT wasn't so bad.
So...the next day or two...
It was NEW.
I took that back to that Top Value place.
An⌐ I said, "Say." I said,
"There's a little something wrong with this ZIPPER."
Had her back in the case, you know.
And the girl said, "Oh," said, "What's the number on
**   that?"**
She looked...
Said, "Well we've got another one back here."
Said, "Just give me that and I'll give you a NEW one."
Took her back and I told Wally, I said, "Well that
wasn't   so bad.
I said, "They give me a brand new...brand new..."
Esther: UMBRELLA.
Jack: Well I was comin' to that.
Ledell: That's a different STORY.

The women are all laughing now; men are slapping their legs and chuckling. Jack begins the next story...which everyone knows is coming.

Jack: So THEN.
On the umbrella.
She gave me a new UMBRELLA for Christmas one
**   time.**
Never had used it.

It was one of them you just flip a button, you know, and
  boy (slaps hands) she'd go right up and boy it was
  really HANDY...
Pulled her back down. (Jack illustrates)
So I had that up in Indianapolis
(Spiv laughs out loud at this setting).
And we was goin' up there on Pennsylvania Street to a
  restaurant.
Man just a-pourin' down rain.
And I got up there and went to pull that umbrella down
  and she wouldn't come DOWN.
She was locked open.
Well you couldn't leave it on Pennsylvania Street cause
it   was gonna blow away, or somebody'd STEAL it.
(everyone is chuckling)
So there I was...
Well...when I was tryin' to pull that down
Candid Camera had gone off the air, but I thought it'd
  come back on cause I looked around for somebody
to   be...some news reporter to be takin' my PICTURE
  tryin' to get that down.
And so I told the boys...I said, "Well go on in there and
  get us a table. I'll take this back to the City-County
  Building."
So it was two blocks...
Back to the City-County Building.
Couldn't get it through that revolving-door part cause
  it was still open see.
(Spiv laughs out loud; the women are giggling)
There was another door you go in.
Well I tried to get through THAT door.
That door was about THAT wide (Jack gestures)...and
  that old umbrella was about THAT wide, see.

I STILL couldn't work her around.

And I finally worked that around and got in and there I
   was inside that building walkin' along there with
   that umbrella up, you know...

(the women are poking fun at Jack during all this)

Everybody lookin' at me...and I went down to the
   garage...where the CAR was parked.

(the women are laughing out loud now at the tale's
coming end)

And I thought...

"Well I can't get her YET."

So I just took her like THAT, you know (illustrates).

And I just BROKE every one of them things

And I just folded her up and laid her in the truck.

Esther is "oooohhing," Spiv is laughing out loud,
everyone is cracking up at Jack's story. But there is more to
come. As soon as we settle down, Jack continues.

Now this was in March...

A YEAR later than...

Not just three MONTHS after Christmas but a YEAR
   and three months after Christmas.

So on the way home at Dalton and Payne I just whirled
   in there that evening you know...and went in there.

(women are chuckling)

   And I was looking around...pickin' these umbrellas
   up and lookin', you know...

And I had that old one there a-carryin' it you know...

And that guy said, "Can I HELP you?"

And I said, "Yeah I think you can..."

I said "My wife got me a new umbrella here for
   Christmas."

(Jack pauses and the women giggle)
And I said, "It wouldn't WORK."
And I said, "There it IS."
He said, "Oh yeah. We've had a LOT of trouble with
     them."
He said, "Just pick you OUT one there."
(The women are laughing loudly now and the men
chuckling and slapping their legs.)
He took that and I picked out one.
Come on home.
I come in and I says, "See...I got a new UMBRELLA."
And she said,
(low gruff voice) "You didn't TELL him that...
     it just BROKE."
I said, "I did NOT tell him."
I said you got that for Christmas.
And I said, 'It hasn't worked right. It's broke'...and he
     just said, 'Help yourself'..."
(The women are laughing loudly here)
And I didn't TELL him...
(everyone is cracking up now)
Marybelle: And this is the convener of the session...at
     the church!
(burst of even louder women's laughter at this)
Jack: Now can you see where I LIED or anything on
     that?
Spiv: Bad as old Dave RUFF (apparently in reference to
     local liar everyone has heard about)
Sally: He just made it EASY for ya.
Jack: Just made it easy.

Folks continue to tease Jack and work over the tale for a
while, then the women begin to remember other cases

they've heard of outlandish returning of merchandise. Esther and Margueritte, Margaret, Ledell each have their brief episodes to recount.

Conversations float back and forth across the room. The men withdraw into some private topics and the women start up their own conversations.

At 9:30 P.M. Jeff must leave to report to work at his job of night auditor/night desk clerk at a huge motel in Columbus. Everyone questions him about his job, the motel, the New Year's Eve plans at the hotel. He supplies all the answers genially and leaves amid a round of farewells. "Drive carefully." It's New Year's Eve and the drunks will be out. The various conversations continue. At 10 P.M. Bill Byford says, "Jeff is at work by now."

Wally, Jack, and Nolan begin to tell of school-day antics. Jack gets onto school bus-driving problems. Nolan, Jack, and Spiv had all driven a school bus at one time or another...and Wally had ridden them plenty. Everyone listens and laughs as they tell story after story.

Jack: Well I know Dad, he drove a school bus and he had Wes Barringer and Charlie Elsie...
And most of the time...he'd let them out at the red barn up here.
Because they'd holler.
And just as soon as they'd holler...well then Dad'd let them out.
And they could WALK home.

Spiv chuckles at this and the women laugh lightly. It seems like school bus discipline was plenty strict in those days.

Jack goes on: So they probably walked more than they
ever rode on Dad's bus.
Aw I can remember...I'd be a kid ridin' up there then.
I can remember Dad'd STOP that old bus. Man.
And I mean TAKE that big old CRANK that opened
the back door.
Take that thing and WHIRL that thing forward and
that back door would open...
Course you'd go out that little side...come back in here.

Sometimes they wouldn't want to get out.
And I've seen Dad grab them by the back of the neck
and drag them all the way back out.
Throw 'em out that step.
Shut that door.
(The women laugh approvingly at Frank McConnell's
stern usage of those unruly boys.)

The conversation pauses a moment while the men
explain to me about the way the school bus door opened at
the back in those days.

Jack concludes: That's really the only two boys I think
ever caused him any trouble.

Nolan remembers school bus *riding* days:

Nolan: Poor old Cress Miller.
Ever time he crossed that Sand Crick bridge...?
He'd slow down to five miles an hour to see what the
water looked like.
(The women laugh and comment)
Nolan: He'd slow down to five mile an hour and he'd

(Nolan mimics Cress taking a long necked gander at the
water over the bridge's sides. His acting brings the
women into gales of laughter.)
...LOOK at the water...
Go through that bridge...
And...
"Here we go." (Off up the hill. The imagery is clear to
the audience, well acquainted with the Sand Creek
bridge. Everyone laughs. Cress Miller was known as a
dedicated fisherman. His checking the water made
sense.)
Sally completes the story: Twice a day, huh.
Nolan: Oh yeah.
He always slowed down to check that water.
See what it looked like.
(The audience chuckles, coughs, clears its throat and
settles down to wait for the next story.)

Jack has another story of his Dad's school bus driving
days. A big boy had caused him some trouble. Frank
banned the boy from the bus until further orders. The boy's
father was to be reckoned with, however, so Frank laid a
two by four in the bus alongside his seat the next morning
when he drove his route...just in case. He didn't need it.

Nolan tells of a kid on a motorbike who gave him
trouble one time when he drove the school bus. Then Jack
launches into what must be one of his classic stories.

Jack: Well the only one that ever caused me any trouble
when I sub drove...was Branstetter.
(The name Branstetter is greeted with loud laughter
and a flurry of comments.)

First grader.

Spiv had the mumps one morning and Esther called
over there.

Said, "Will you drive Spiv's BUS?"

And, Hell, I didn't even know his ROUTE. (Jack
chuckles at the confusing situation.)

I knew where he went.

I knew he went up Devil's Ridge up there, see.

And Esther told me.

Go up there to Branstetter's and turn around and come
back.

And I'd pick up the Branstetter boy first and then I thin
Grizards.

(Spiv and the others comment on this and get it
straight.)

Jack continues: So I went up there the first morning,
you know...turned that bus around.

(The women are muttering among themselves about the
story)

Jack: I know I've told this before.

And...the little Branstetter boy he started out, you
know.

Spiv: He was slow ANYHOW.

Jack: And SLOW.

He just took steps this long. (Jack measures with his
hands)

He was a first grader.

Esther, supporting Branstetter: "Well he was just a
little..."

Jack: Little bitty feller.

He come back around that bus, you know.

And of course he never looked up.

I opened the door.

And I said, "Good morning, young man."
And he looked up there at me, you know...
(Jack lowers his voice)
Just turned around and went back.
(The women burst into laughter at this point)
Spiv: BACK to the house he went!

Jack: Well I looked at my watch.
I'd been fifteen minutes and I haven't even picked up a
    BOY.
Don't know where I'm GOIN'.
Just know I'm headin' fer Scipio.
Well in a little bit his mom come out, you know.
I said, "You're gonna have to help me.
Your bus driver's sick."
I told her, "I said Mr. Helt's...sick.
I'm gonna be drivin' a day or two.
I'm gonna need some...?"
I told HIM, I said, "I'm gonna need some HELP
You're gonna have to tell me where to STOP."
So she got him on.
We went down there and picked up Grizards
And then they told me and we went on in.

So the next morning I told Ledell
I said, "Well I'm gonna leave fifteen minutes earlier this
    morning because..."
(the rest of Jack's sentence is covered in laughter as
everyone cracks up. He's off to pick up Branstetter
again.)

So.
Went back up.

Turned around.
Set there.
Had that light on, you know.
And old Branstetter...I saw him comin', you know.
Come on around.
Come there.
Opened the door.
I said, "Good morning, Young Man."
And he looked up and said
(Jack lowers his voice to a resigned dry tone)
"Forgot my pencil."
(The audience bursts into laughter)
Went back to the house.
Got that pencil.
Come back around.
Got back on.
Well that was another fifteen minutes.
(Jack chuckles, letting the story down)
Till we took off.

The story is over but Jack lets the audience down gently with a bit more commentary about Branstetter. He shakes his head in amazement at the memory.

That was the cutest little guy I ever seen in my life. But I'm tellin' you...that first morning when I said, "Good morning, Young Man."...and he seen I wasn't no SPIV...Man, I mean...they wasn't SIX PEOPLE could have put him on that BUS.

Everyone laughs again. The men are slapping their legs in enjoyment and having a good time over this story.

"Turned right around and went BACK" one of them recapitulates the story.

Spiv remembers: He had a pretty mother too.
Jack: Oh Yes. I was willing to take my TIME.
I wasn't in no hurry.
(This prompts another flurry of joking comments)
Jack: I think Spiv went early.
I think he had coffee there ever morning.
He never told me about that.
(Jack thinks a moment)
And he was cute
And then the next morning, he said...
(in his low dry voice again) "Forgot my PENCIL."
(The women laugh once more. There is a pause.)
Jack: I remember that kid...
up at the Alumnae when he graduated.
I think he was there that time...
I forget just when it was.
Esther: You should've told that.
Jack: I should of.
I thought about it at the time.
Spiv: Whatever become of them?

No one knows for sure quite where the Branstetters are now. Pert thinks they moved over around Garden City or Wellsboro.

The conversation winds off in different directions, leaving the group storytelling event behind. People rearrange themselves around the rooms and small group conversations form and re-form. Laurie, Wally's twenty year old daughter arrives and a flurry of warm greetings rise "Hello Laurie!" "Come on in!" "We've got a *chair* waitin' for you!" calls Margueritte, "Right over *here*." Most women have moved to the kitchen at this point and are carrying on a conversation out there.

This is basically a teetotalling group. Gordon keeps 8 oz. beers in the refrigerator and drinks one now and then. He dislikes pop and feels it is bad for you. Most of the men will have a beer on occasion but alcohol isn't a very important part of their lives. It goes without saying that the women do not drink at all.

The beverage of the evening on this New Year's Eve is iced fruit punch. Still it *is* New Year's Eve...and in keeping with the festive nature of the event Bill brings out a bottle of his own wine and offers a taste around. Such homemade wine is not in the same class as liquor or beer. It has its roots in the remembered traditions of the community's past. The previous generation knew how to make good dandelion wine. Wally remembers his father's elderberry wine.

It is about 10:30 and after a couple of hours of talk all the men have suddenly realized they are thirsty.

Jack starts it off: Pert I'm driern' a fish!

Spiv offers a glass of water.

Jack: Well that's for flowers ain't it?

Someone calls from the kitchen: Bring your *glass*, Jack.

    We've got water in here.

Jack fusses jokingly: Need something stronger than water.

Spiv laughs and teases: That old Jack's drinkin' again.

    Wally realizes he is thirsty too and calls to Bill in the kitchen to bring him a glass.Pert and Jack have gone out to get themselves a glass of water or punch.

Bill comes in with his bottle of homemade wine.

"Would anybody like to have my wine?"

Someone inquires about its origin.
Jack is disgusted: *Now* he asks me...just after I carry
that   in. (He's just come back with a tall glass of
punch.)
Wally: I'll have a little homemade wine.
Several of the men agree to try a little.
Jack breaks in: Hey I got one other question for ya.
You said homemade wine...
Where's George Bannister buried at?
Spiv laughs loudly and the other men join in.
(George Bannister was famous for his love of wine.)

Spiv takes some wine: I don't know what it *is*...but I'll
    take a little.
Jack asks Bill: Where'd you *hurt* that at Bill? Who
made it?
All sip the wine and give their approval.
Spiv: That's pretty good wine.

In the kitchen Margueritte is not exactly pleased. Bill
has gotten out the little glasses to serve his wine in.
Margueritte starts to comment on the little glasses, perhaps
to say that they should be washed before using, but gives it
up and turns to the women in a dry undertone. "They're
gonna drink wine." The women shift a bit, disapprovingly.
They'd just as soon the men *didn't*. But then it *is* New
Year's Eve. They resume their conversations.

Nolan upends his glass and utters a toast!

"Up the mouth and over the gums
Look out stomach, here she comes!"

Conversation turns to other matters. The evening's drinking is done with.

At 11:30 people begin to get up and move back toward the table for a bite more. The table had been partially covered to keep things fresh all this time. Now the plastics have been removed, the deviled egg trays refilled, the baked beans reheated. No one eats much now though. Only a couple even bother to pick up another plate and fill it. Just a nibble here or there at the finger food seems adequate at this late hour.

At ten minutes till midnight the TV is turned on and all sit and watch Times Square drop the New Year's ball. The Pointer Sisters are singing and jiggling while the nation waits. The men stand and stare. The women tease them to sit down and let them see. The one teen age girl in the house dances a couple of steps to herself as she watches and several adults make teasing comments not disapprovingly "Look at her go!" She stops right away and retreats from the room.

Promptly at midnight the TV ball drops into Times Square. Spiv stares unsmiling at the TV screen. Esther shouts, " Happy New Year," and lifts an arm in cheer. Nolan does the same thing twice or three times. Everyone else sits and watches. They call rather unconvincingly, "Happy New Year" or, "Hooray." Nine year old Julie, who had been afraid the room would just sit talking right past midnight without even *noticing* the New Year waves her arms in the air and calls, "Hooray!" I snap a few photos, mainly of Spiv staring at the TV.

Everyone seemed quite satisfied with the event. There was no rush to go home but within fifteen minutes folks were on their feet, locating winter coats from the bedroom where they had been tossed on a bed and moving toward the back door to leave. Everyone thanked Margueritte again for the marvelous feast and the nice evening and left. The "young" crew consisting of Wally, Jack, and Nolan helped Sally out to the car, pushed Laura's car out of its snow pile, and collected their own wives to leave. By 12:30 A.M. we were all gone home. Margueritte had a kitchen full of food to refrigerate and a sink full of dirty dishes to do. At 12:45 A.M. their furnace broke again.

*   *   *

Well that was New Year's Eve in Scipio. Not too exciting, you might say. Yet completely satisfying to the folks in Scipio. The evening was satisfying because it was a well-executed group play. Everyone knew his part, everyone performed well. And all took part in the evening's entertainment. To understand why this last statement is true, let's examine the role of the audience in Scipio storytelling.

CHAPTER 2
HOW TO LISTEN TO A STORY IN SCIPIO

ROLE OF THE AUDIENCE

Storytelling sessions in Scipio seem clearly to be a form of group play. Each member of the audience plays his or her part. Successful storytelling requires not only a skillful teller, but also a skilled audience. A careful look at the Scipio audience shows them constantly in tune with their tellers, carefully reinforcing, encouraging, and playing their own roles in the evening's verbal melee.

It may seem that the audience is simply relaxing and responding to the stories in a random fashion, but a close examination of an evening of friends visiting and swapping stories shows definite patterns of response. The audience obviously knows their role well and is consistent in the way they respond to and reinforce the storyteller.(1)

* * *

BEFORE THE TALE BEGINS

Conversation seldom begins with the "story." It begins with "talk" and meanders from topic to topic until something reminds someone of a story. If the prospective teller is a master narrator and if the story is one the teller considers particularly good, the teller will probably turn from his own conversational group and offer it to the whole room.

Throughout the evening multiple two or three person conversations were carried on around the living room and in the kitchen. After each story, if no other story was forthcoming right away, the multiple conversations would break out again and continue until another story began. But as soon as a storyteller started to narrate...the multiple conversations would break off and attention would focus on the new storyteller. The prospective audience at all times had one ear out for any new storytelling event that might break out. They seemed particularly attuned to the two men in the room most likely to start a story...Spiv and Jack.

Those tellers, then, who were *expected* to offer stories did not have to collect the room's attention before beginning their narration. They simply started narrating and by the end of the second sentence of their narration, the room had usually quieted down.

DURING THE TELLING

Audience Reinforcement

The Scipio telling is best understood when viewed as a group play rather than as monologue performance. Most members of the audience are actively participating throughout the telling session. All position themselves in an active listening stance, and contribute laughter, approving vocalization, or comments throughout the story.

There is a slight difference in the audience reinforcement provided by the women and that of the men. The women are more vocal in their laughter. Throughout the telling the women reinforce the male teller by letting out little bursts of laughter, chuckling, and making teasing comments which poke fun at the teller as he goes along.

The male listeners provide reinforcement by their attention and eager listening stance...their laughter, however, is more often a quiet chuckle. In this group only Spiv lets out an occasional loud guffaw, Jack an occasional cackle.(2) Audible reinforcement is provided by comments both during and after the telling. An occasional loud knee slap or hand clap marks high points in the telling, while the accompanying male laughter remains an almost inaudible chuckle.

Tale Jumping

If the story has been heard before, as was the case in this evening's telling, both men and women will begin to chime in with knowledgeable jumps on the story throughout the telling.(3) Spiv: "And then he..." Pert: "*Sat* on it." Spiv: "Sat on it."

This kind of group involvement in the telling seems important to the group enjoyment of the tale and "jumping" the story *reinforces* the teller rather than annoying. In fact, stories which invoke such audience involvement seem to provide the most enjoyment for the group.(4) The audience will also jump stories heard for the first time, if the plot provides an obvious denouement.

Tale jumping and the interjection of comments at certain junctures within the tale and at the tale's end are a requirement of listeners in the Scipio conversational setting. By such continued verbal support of the teller, the audience reaffirms throughout the narration that they are still "with him", they are all still "playing the conversational game." A speaker whose story fell into a void lacking in verbal response might begin to feel uncomfortable, as if his narrative were being ill-received by the group. He might let the narrative dwindle away and drop the topic.(5)

Even the few individuals in the Scipio community who are of a taciturn personality style, have adapted to the conversational game well.(6) They make contributory jumps just as do the more hyperactive conversational members. Their jumps are lower in key, offered quietly and somewhat less frequently than the jumps of a star player such as Jack McConnell or Spiv Helt, but they are right in there affirming their presence in the game through continued verbal support, as required by the rules of the game. They are, however, unlikely to jump another person's conversation by introducing a topic of their own. These jumps are more of the appreciative and encouraging type.

AFTER THE TELLING

The punch line in Scipio stories is only the *beginning* of the end. It arrives in a wrapping up which has probably already begun to spawn jumps and audience comments. After its skillful delivery, there is a slight pause usually followed by a humorous reinforcing phrase from the audience, followed by a repetition of the punch line by the teller.(7) Other humorous reinforcing comments from the audience proliferate, usually all at once, covering each other after each joke ending.

This tradition seems to rely as much on audience performance style as on the teller's performance style. The audience is waiting with bated breath...ready to chime in with commentary and extend the joke as soon as the punch line is delivered. The extended ending of this type of tale delivery is a group tradition as well as a stylistic device of the teller.

The teller may then follow with another brief recap of the tale's ending, or other illustrative commentary about the tale...extending the joke as it were and invoking another round of laughter.(8)

The proliferation of joking behavior following the tale's ending is usually allowed to die down by itself before any other topic is introduced into the conversation. This is especially true if the story just told is a particularly funny one, provoking hearty laughter. Gradually the laughter and chuckling die away, comments cease, throats are cleared, a few coughs heard, and perhaps a few weary sighs. Then silence lies peacefully on the room. Only after this restful pause to enjoy has passed will another teller start up a tale.

To jump in with another topic of conversation or the next story before the first tale has been allowed to reap its reward in expired laughter and sighs would be as rude as interrupting *during* the story. The story, in other words, is not actually finished until the last appreciative sigh has been breathed.

It is clear that storytelling in Scipio is a group effort. No one feels bored or left out in a Scipio story performance because everyone is taking part...laughing, teasing the teller, tossing out humorous asides. Folks don't **stop** the talking when a master teller starts up...they *begin.*(9) The amount of kibitzing in the room probably increases in direct proportion to the skill of the teller holding the floor. Not that the skilled teller won't command spots of absolute silence, and the master teller has the skills to claim such spots. But the general tone of the happy storytelling event is one of group participation.(10)

NOTES
CHAPTER 2:

1.   Annette Powell Williams points out the importance of properly interpreting audience response in her "Dynamics of a Black Audience." In *Rappin' and Stylin' Out: Communication in Urban Black America,* ed. Thomas Kochman (Urbana: University of Illinois Press, 1972), pp.102-106.

2.   The most aggressive storytellers provided the most audible laugh response for other tellers.

3.   For discussion of several other kinds of simul-talk, see the summary of research on simultaneous talk in Margaret L. McLaughlin, *Conversation: How Talk is Organized* (Beverly Hills: Sage Publications, 1984). McLaughlin discusses speech overlap and interruption in the changing of turns in speech, (pp. 122-130) and discusses backchannel utterances (acknowledgements like "uh-huh" or "yeah" made during another's speech) as a *symbolic* claim to a turn (pp. 102-103).

4.   Karl Reisman in his article "Contrapuntal Conversations in a Antiguan Village," (ed. Richard Bauman and Joel Sherzer. *Explorations in the Ethnography of Speaking* (London: Cambridge University Press, 1974), pp. 110-124 discusses a simultaneous talk situation in which it is proper for everyone to say whatever they wish to say without waiting for a turn. The multi-conversations keep up until each speaker either gets his point across or gives up. His term "contrapuntal conversation" seems apt for Scipio's constant stream of supportive comments as well.

5.   For just a few examples of the importance of audience reinforcement to storytelling see: Ilhan Basgoz, "The Tale Singer and His Audience." in Dan Ben-Amos and Kenneth Goldstein, *Folklore, Communication and Performance* (The Hague: Mouton, 1975), pp.

153-192; Bruce Rosenburg, *The Art of the American Folk Preacher* (Palo Alto: Stanford University Press, 1970); and J. Barre Toelken "The 'Pretty Language' of Yellow Man: Genre, Mode and Texture in Navaho Coyote Narratives" in *Folklore Genres*, ed. Dan Ben-Amos (Austin: University of Texas Press, 1976), pp. 145-170.

6.   This cultural habit of "jumping" stories can be interpreted as a personality flaw when used inappropriately outside of a story-jumping cultural setting. My entire paternal family, whose adults all were raised in Southern Indiana, carries on this kind of rapid conversational patter complete with incessant "jumps" by listeners. To my husband, raised in a family structure of taciturn men, who are slow to come to speech and very respectful of each other's verbal space, our entire family seems rude and inconsiderate. He refuses to play the conversational game with us. Whenever *his* speech is "jumped" he stops talking and withdraws. And since he refuses to jump our speech, he never gets a word in edgewise.

7.   James Leary comments on this extended tale-ending format in his notes on Wisconsin Polish teller Max Trzebiatowski. "Max's punchlines, when present, were not final utterances, bang-up endings after which nothing more could be said, but words to savor or repeat, preludes to further commentary and discussion. James Leary, "The Favorite Jokes of Max Trzebiatowski," p. 7 *in Humor and the Individual*. California Folklore Society, 1984.

Gershon Legman comments similarly on Vance Randolph's Ozark tellers. "Practically all of his one hundred tales, outfitted though most of them are with punchlines, do not stop at the verbal climax, but continue on with some homey moralizing or droll observation, often a paragraph in length." Gershon Legman, *The Horn Book: Studies in Erotic Folklore and Bibliography* (New Hyde Park, New York: University Books, 1964), p. 491.

8.   Simon J. Bronner in "Saturday Night in Greenville: An Interracial Tale and Music Session in Context" *Folklore Forum*, 14, No. 2, (1981): 85-120 notes that "Both Eugene and George like to repeat punch lines of jokes after a rendition in order to stimulate further laughter." p. 112.

9.   Edelsky (C. Edelsky, "Who's Got the Floor?" *Language in Society*, 10, (1981), pp. 383-421) posits two kinds of conversational floor. She described F1 as an orderly, one-at-a-time type in which people took fewer, but longer, turns; there was more frequent use of the past tense; there was a greater use of the reporting function; and there were more side comments and encouragers. F2 was characterized by an apparent

free for all, the collaborative building of a single idea. F2's had more turns that shared the same meaning; more laughing, joking, and teasing; more "deep" overlapping; little apparent concern for interruption; and more topics on which more than one participant was informed. pp. 106-107.

In Scipio, official meetings are conducted according to F1 criteria. Casual conversational gatherings revert to F2 style. It might even be useful to propose a third conversational floor, "F3," to describe the floor during storytelling itself. Once a storyteller "takes the floor" interruption is no longer feasible, but attentive body language and back-channel comment and vocalization are *required* of the sensitive listener. The conversational rules applicable during the story narration are quite different from those at work during the "free for all" interludes between the stories. In the "free for all" periods interruptions and simultaneous talk are expected. Full attention and accompanying back channel response are not required, though back channel chatter certainly does proliferate.

10. Bruce Rosenburg draws similar conclusions for the congregation of the folk preacher. "Not only is he, by his active participation in the service, influencing the preacher in several ways, but he is creating a personal religious experience, and expressing it while the rest of the congregation are creating theirs. They are all a part of the sermon, and every bit as much as is the preacher." Bruce Rosenburg, *The Art of the American Folk Preacher* (New York: Oxford University Press, 1970), p. 105.

CHAPTER 3
HOW TO TELL A STORY IN SCIPIO: DELIVERY AND RELATIONSHIP TO AUDIENCE

The New Year's Eve 1984 storying sequence gives us a chance to see a Scipio audience in action. It also gives us a chance to see several different tellers perform. Just about everyone in Scipio knows how to tell a good story.(1)Let's take a look at how they do it.

THE PERFORMERS

The performance styles of the men tellers in this group are very similar. All of the men tell humorous anecdotal stories at one time or another. The tellers who step forth in large gatherings such as this New Year's Eve party can be considered the group's *master* tellers. Spiv Helt, an acknowledged master teller of the group, was mostly silent this night. He is 84 and it is hard for him to hear in a crowded room. Jack McConnell took the floor and held it well for most of the evening. Wally Hines and Nolan

Spencer both showed skill at relating stories but offered only brief episodes this evening. Pert Helt can tell a story well enough but usually keeps quiet and lets his brother Spiv do the telling when they are in the same group. Bill Byford, the evening's host, sat quietly in a chair and let the others offer the evening's entertainment. The Byford's grandsons Jeff and Scott, in their early twenties, did not attempt to enter the storytelling arena. Except for a couple anecdotes performed by myself and an anecdote told by Sally Helt, the women confined their storytelling activities to small groups of women.

It is interesting, when looking at this evening's storytelling, to look at those anecdotes which were *not* performed as well as those which *were* performed.

Though most members of the group did not try to hold the entire group with a story, everyone was conversing throughout the evening. Folks who did not *want* to tell their story to the whole group would begin an anecdote they wished to relate by turning to a conversational partner and relating the story in a quiet voice. Some of the anecdotes shared in this manner were similar in content to those performed for the group by the master tellers.

Of the conversation carried on within range of my tape recorder on this New Year's Eve, Jack provided thirteen structured stories, one play sequence about the zippered walls, and two non-structured gossip segments of some length. Spiv offered three structured stories; Nolan four brief structured segments; Wally four. Bill Byford told one structured tale about a mole in his yard but directed it to his conversational partner and let the room's conversation cover it before it was finished. As a guest, I told two structured narratives and in response to questions, offered a lengthy description of Mt. St. Helen's activity. Sally gave one structured narrative. Jeff talked at length about New Year's Eve at his motel when prodded by questioners. Esther showed and talked about her "Scipio Switchblade" (a joke item made of clothespins and rubber bands which flung open like a switchblade knife when held a certain way).

These are the only conversational offerings of any length which dominated the entire living room during that evening.

Despite the fact that Jack obviously monopolized the floor when it came to storytelling, no one felt that Jack talked too much, or that they had not had a chance to take part. This is true because everyone was talking practically all of the time. They were chatting quietly with their conversational partners, or if silenced by a narrator who was drawing the attention of the entire group...then commenting continually on his/her narration. Storytelling in Scipio is not monologue performance, it is group play.

THE TELLER'S RELATIONSHIP TO HIS AUDIENCE

We have talked about the audience's responsibilities during a tale telling, now let's take a look at the responsibilities of the teller.(2) It is up to the teller to entertain, amuse, and guide the audience through the tale-telling event. Tellers use a variety of delivery techniques to achieve these aims, but before examining the teller's techniques for delivery, it might be useful to look more closely at the exact nature of the relationship between teller and audience. We have seen that in Scipio storytelling the audience plays an active part, creating moments of "group play" in the storytelling event. To execute this, the master teller must hold a close rapport with his audience. He must read well their moods and potential for play.

Barre Toelken refers to a "contractual agreement" between teller and audience. They agree to cooperate in producing this "event" with certain mutual expectations of each other and for the event they hope to achieve.(3)

Tale Selection and Timing of Offering

The master teller's rapport with the group enables him to select just the right tale for the group's mood, and to offer it at precisely the most auspicious moment for reception by the group.(4)

This skill also helps the teller assess just how much story a group can take. Should he cut it short, stretch it out...run on into another tale...or give it a rest for a while.

Caretaking the Audience

A talent for "audience caretaking" is probably the single most important skill of the "master" storyteller.(5) The teller may use many techniques to soothe, amuse, excite, and control his audience. But his careful attention to their needs is paramount. He must know just where they are at all times...when they need to breathe, to laugh, to cry, to exclaim. He must cue into his own telling the reactions that the audience needs to make.

Every audience wants to collaborate with their teller in the creation of an aesthetic event. They *want* to be a good audience, to feel the joy of having shared in an artistic creation - the perfectly told tale.

It is the "master" teller who knows how to lead his audience, to guide them into a perfect accompaniment to his performance, to help them *be* a good audience. He does this with his skilled pacing, pause, wording, attack, voice tone, body language, eye contact. He directs his audience much as a conductor directs an orchestra. And if he plays them well, the artistic creation feels good. It is a source of pride to both the teller and audience. They created together this story event.(6)

Charisma

It is possible that charisma, that nebulous factor so difficult to explain, may be largely a result of skillful audience caretaking. The charismatic individual is one who makes us feel we have performed well as audience.

DELIVERY

Now let us turn to the specific delivery techniques in Scipio. Some of the techniques for story delivery which are used by Scipio storytellers are:

* A straightforward, confident beginning to a tale.
* Use of parallel structure (including alliteration)
* Varied pacing and the dramatic pause.
* Varied voice tone, mimicry.
* Fitting of narrative style to content.
* Narrative-directed body language.
* Ending the tale assuredly.
* Capping the tale.

A Straightforward, Confident Beginning to the Tale

In order to be assured of his audience's attention, the teller must signal immediately that he is launching into a "performance." This is not just more talk. In a few moments we will discuss the textual elements which facilitate this keying, but more important than the text's keys, the *performative* features of the teller's first utterance seem important in capturing his audience.(7)

Pregnant Pause: A pregnant pause is effective, but in a room full of chattering would-be tellers use of the pregnant pause may be risky. Someone else may mistake it for an opportunity to speak. Body language, however, can hold a pause, especially for the skilled master teller whose ways are familiar to the group.

Attack: The first sentence must be attacked assuredly. It must be stated clearly. And it must proceed to its completion without hesitation and with a clear sense of pacing.

Pacing: A rhythmic opening with clear stresses helps signal performance and collect the audience's attention. An examination of six opening lines from the 1985 New Year's Eve party will illustrate. (We will visit that party in Chapter 4). The tellers were swapping first-smoke stories here. Since the narratives from which these opening sentences were taken were all thrown into the ring during an open-tale telling session, they illustrate well the pattern used by male tellers in need of capturing the floor.

First Sentences Marked for Stress:

Wally: Went down to Hayden
     when Clyde and I was pretty small.

Wally #2: Clyde and I went over there one day.

Tom: I knew the first time I ever got sick...was on
     cigarettes.

Bill: I never did get sick on cigarettes...but I did on a chew of tobaccer.

Jack: I got sick on old...chewin' tobacco...and an old stub cigar.

Wally: We was down there at the Nettle Creek Bridge one day.

In each case the rhythmic nature of these opening sentences helped gather the attention of the room and elicit a readiness for story.

The Master Teller's Prerogative

Group members with a known repertoire of tales will often be asked to recount a certain episode. "Tell the one about the time..." The teller will usually chuckle appreciatively at the choice of tale, glance around the room at the expectant audience...and launch into the story.

One of the group's master tellers, however, can begin a tale at any point in the evening's conversation *without* bothering to gain the attention of the group first. The teller will already be engaged in conversation with one or two other men, while the other folks in the room are conversing in isolated small groups. The master teller begins his tale by raising his voice and addressing himself to the group as a whole rather than to his conversation partner. The other conversational groups will usually drop their own talk immediately and turn to the master teller so as to not miss a word of his story.(8) No one feels that he has *interrupted* the other conversations. They just stopped talking in order to hear him. During the New Year's Eve 1984 party, this technique was employed several times to gain the attention of the group for a story.

Nor are master tellers daunted by a failure to capture the group's attention on the first try.

Jack begins: "The reason I want..."

Not enough folks are paying attention so he pauses...and begins again...in exactly the same wording and intonation. This time he gains the floor and proceeds.

The Key Listener: Another trick employed by the would- be teller is that of capturing first the attention of a "key listener." Jack might begin a story by addressing Spiv..."Spiv, you might not have heard this one." With Spiv's attention on Jack, the rest of the room is easy to capture. Folklorists have spent some time studying "key informants" but the "key listener" may also deserve some attention.

Use of Parallel Structure Including Alliteration

I discuss parallel tale structure here as well as with a discussion of the tale text since much of its parallelism is achieved through pacing of the delivery. The text seems to truncate itself to follow the tale's pace, rather than the other way around.

Tellers are adept at using parallel structures to produce an aesthetically pleasing tale.(9) Jack showed a conscious use of parallel structure when he began his story of the suitcase. "You couldn't buy..." then stopped and began again, expanding the phrase to the formulaic, alliterative..."You couldn't buy, beg, borry or steal..." Jack spoke each word resonantly, keeping them on the same tone to emphasize the alliterative sounds and the parallel effect.

Nolan uses parallel phrasing in his description of Crescent Miller crossing the Sand Creek bridge driving the school bus.

He'd SLOW down to five miles an hour
    and he'd (acts out Cress eyeballing the Sand Creek
    waters from the bus window)...
LOOK at that water...
GO through that bridge...
And...HERE WE GO!

By omitting conjunctions, refusing to repeat pronouns, and cutting the narrative to brief action lines...the story achieves a pleasing parallel form.

Spiv uses this stylistic device frequently in his narration. Of hired man Old Tom Read, he says:

He'd mow that yard, you know...
Keep that yard mowed...
Weeds cut back...
Hoein' the garden...
Cuttin' the wood...
Split wood...
Cord wood...
Build fence...
Just such stuff as that.

In listing a chain of events or a list of items, the conjunctions and repeated pronouns are often dropped for stylistic effect. Even if the conjunctions are retained, the dramatic pause between each word or phrase and the forceful delivery which gives each phrase the value of a sentence itself, creates a parallel structure. This structure reveals itself when transcriptions show speech pauses.

Spiv tells about starting out to farm:

Well I'd saved a LITTLE bit of money.
And it didn't TAKE any THEN.
I bought...
A tractor.
And a wagon.
A disk.
Cultivator.
And a corn planter.
And it seemed to me like...it was a thousand...and a few
     dollars...
For the whole WORKS.

Alliteration

When alliteration occurs in Scipio speech it often seems more a function of performance than text. Jack McConnell begins his sentence "You couldn't buy..." then stops and begins again, launching into full performance with forceful stress on each initial "B" to create a pleasing show of alliteration "You couldn't *buy, beg, borry* or *steal...*"

Varied Pacing and the Dramatic Pause

As we have seen, the teller's use of pacing can create a parallel effect in his narration. Pacing is used both to create a poetic, rhythmic swing to speech, to place effect and to exercise control over the audience. It is also used to catch your breath.

In the segment which follows notice how skillfully Jack uses the dramatic pause to take his audience just where he wants them.

Jack tells of breaking the zipper on his suitcase:

So we got ready to open that up...(he pauses to create suspense)
and it got caught.
And I worked on it you know.
I stayed cool. (Jack is stylizing his speech with calm, short sentences)
Didn't want to get maad...or nothin' like that.
(Jack stretches "maad" sarcastically...to make his joke)
People around there ,you know.
Well the longer I worked...(Jack pauses again for suspense)
...I got a little bit...(Jack pauses again to set us up for his laugh line)
...UN-tolerant. (By stressing the "un" syllable Jack reinforces the punching of this statement as   "laugh line.")

This is an internal laugh line. Jack stops his speech entirely on this line and it is delivered with a finality that tells the audience it is their turn. They begin at once to toss in comments amidst the laughter following Jack's laugh line.

Esther: Here it comes...
Wally: The redder his face got...
Ledell: His face got red...

Having let his audience have their vocal stretch, enjoy their laugh, and catch up...Jack takes control again and goes on with his story.

Skillful use of the pause is an important factor in "taking care" of an audience. They must be given time to laugh, given a chance to chime in with their own accumulated comments, time to catch up and get ready for the laugh that lies ahead.

Varied Voice Tone, Mimicry

Jack McConnell's umbrella story is a good example of varied voice within a story. Jack begins by narrating in his usual "Jack telling a story" tone. When he enters the store to exchange the umbrella his voice assumes a very polite tone. Back home he speaks to his wife in his normal "everyday Jack" tone. She replies in the low, gruff voice of a mortified conspirator. "You didn't *tell* him that...it just *broke*." Jack's voice turns indignant at once.

"I did NOT tell him."
I said that you got that for Christmas.
And I said, 'It hasn't worked right.
It's broke'...and he just said, 'Help yourself.'"
I said...(Jack suddenly becomes "everyday Jack" again and his laugh line, while ostensibly still a part of his quoted conversation with Ledell, is delivered half to the present audience for THEIR approval.)
I said..."Now he didn't ASK me what Christmas...
And I didn't TELL him."

The telling of the story in a variety of vocal keys and the occasional use of mimicry provides a pleasantly varied listening experience. No one goes to sleep during Jack's stories. They entertain and amuse.

Fitting of Narrative Style to Content

Master tellers are adept at fitting the narrative style, pacing, and voice tone to the particular tale. Jack McConnell is particularly good at this. Notice his use of abrupt phrasing to tell about the plodding actions of little Branstetter, the first grader. In the tale's first episode, Jack had shown how Branstetter took tiny little steps and moved very slowly from house to bus on the first morning Jack sub drove. Now Jack drives up on the second morning. He has left fifteen minutes early this time to allow for Branstetter's slow steps.

So.
Went back up.
Turned around.
Set there.
Had that light on, you know.
And old Branstetter
I saw him comin', you know.
Come on around.
Come there.
Opened the door.
I said, "Good morning, young man."
And he looked up and said,
(lowers voice) "Forgot my pencil." (in resigned tone)
(Jack pauses to allow audience to laugh)
Went back to the house.
Got that pencil.
Come back around.
Got back on.

(pause)
Well that was another fifteen minutes.

Jack's tone throughout is one of plodding resignation, reaching its low point in Branstetter's muttered, "Forgot my pencil," and culminating in Jack's own resigned exclamation at the episode's end. "Well, that was another fifteen minutes."
By contrast Jack's description of breaking the zipper on his daughter's suitcase comes out all in one breath:

Finally when I give that one yank on it there well it come loose.
We just...
Shredded that zipper all the way around it there,
  tore her out of there and just laid her back
  and you could get all the clothes you wanted...

The breathless rapidity of Jack's final statement in the suitcase episode is all the more effective because of the careful pacing of the earlier portion of that story, which had been paced to stress Jack's calm and self-control.

Narrative Directed Body Language
Scipio tellers match their body stance and their use of gesture to their tale. Tales describing excessive action usually involve a certain amount of active demonstration from the teller. Jack McConnell will on occasion leap into the middle of the floor and literally act out his character's actions through a particularly active segment of the tale. He resumes his seat once that bit of explanation has been demonstrated and continues his story.

Most of Scipio's male tellers use hand gestures throughout their telling. But since our tellers were collected on audiotape only, detailed analysis of their use of gesture and physical stance is not possible.

Most tellers make eye contact with audience members at regular intervals throughout tale telling in Scipio but the teller may go for considerable stretches without making eye contact with his audience. He may "enter" his tale as a character, demonstrating motions, quoting conversation, in effect "acting out" portions of the tale on a dramatic plane which does not involve audience eye contact. The head nay be tilted down or away from the audience during delivery of these scenes.

Ending the Tale Assuredly
The effective ending of a tale is created by skillful combination of pause, pacing, voice tone and stress.

Jack ends the umbrella story:

Now he didn't ASK me what Christmas...(stresses the"ask"...pauses for effect)
And I didn't TELL him. (caps the tale off with a brief, stressed line to elicit the laugh)

Capping the Tale
As we saw in our discussion of the audience's responsibilities within the tale performance, a tale is not finished at the punchline. The teller's responsibilities too carry on through the sequence of audience responsibilities and into the rest between stories. The teller is expected to continue to add capping lines, repeat the story's punchline, or carry the joke further with brief comment. The teller

should see his story through with several such utterances until the response murmur dies off.

Jack carries this tradition well at the finish of his umbrella story. The audience erupts into laughter on his laugh line "And I didn't *tell* him."

Marybelle: And this is the convener of the session...at church! (the women crack up over this. Jack lets them go on for a moment.)
Jack: Now can you see where I LIED or anything on that?
Spiv: Bad as old Dave RUFF.
Sally: He just made it easy for ya.
Jack: Just made it easy.
He did...
He said, "Aw we've got a lot of trouble with them,"
He said,
"Just pick you up one," he said.
Esther: You was going to TELL him.
Jack: I was gonna tell him. Yeah.

We have examined a few of the delivery techniques through which the Scipio teller affects his audience: pause, pacing, parallel form, varied voice tone and mimicry, body language, and the fitting of narrative style to content. These combine with a confident attack especially noticeable in the tale's opening and closing and in its internal laugh lines.

Let's visit Scipio for yet another New Year's Eve and then discuss features of the tale text itself.

NOTES
CHAPTER 3

1. The fact that all members of a storying culture know how to structure a tale is mentioned also by Kay L. Cothran in her essay on "Talking Trash in the Okefenokee Swamp Rim, Georgia" *Journal of American Folklore*, 87, no. 346, (Oct-Dec. 1974): 340-356 "A great many men in the rim can talk trash when the occasion for it arises; properly sociable men are expected to be able to do so. Many enliven trash conversation with a clever experience story. Thus competence in talking trash goes hand in hand with the essentials of male sociability," (p. 342).

2. "Performance as a mode of spoken verbal communication consists in the assumption of responsibility to an audience for a display of communicative competence...From the point of view of the audience, the act of expression on the part of the performer is thus marked as subject to evaluation...additionally it is marked as available for the enhancement of experience, through the present enjoyment of the intrinsic qualities of the act of expression itself. Performance thus "gives license to the audience to regard the act of expression and the performer with special intensity," (p. 11). Richard Baumann, *Verbal Art as Performance*. (Prospect Heights, Illinois: Waveland Press, 1977).

3. Barre Toelken, in his discussion of the "recitational devices" used by Yellowman mentions "dramatic intonation," "special nasalized delivery of all vowel sounds," "variation in phrasing," "appropriate gestures, facial expressions, and body positions," "and, very importantly, a kind of contractual interaction which is developed by the narrator with his audience which tends to direct these other aspects of recitation and which seems based in their mutual recognition of the story type, its central characters and their importance in the Navaho world view, and their expectation that this particular performance will cause important ideas to come alive in exciting ways," (pp. 224-225). J. Barre Toelken, "The 'Pretty Language' of Yellowman: Genre, Mode, and Texture in Navaho Coyote Narratives" *Genre* 2, (1969): 211-235.

4. Roger Abrahams notes the importance of this quality in a master teller. "...a master tactician in the game of conversation--to know when to draw on a story, how much time, and by extension, how much elaboration will be tolerated. Gauging such a factor means assessing

what kind of interactional scene you are involved in, as well as what your speaking status is in that scene," (p.11). Roger Abrahams, "The Most Embarrassing Thing That Ever Happened: Conversational Stories in a Theory of Enactment." *Folklore Forum*, 10, No. 3 (Winter 1977): 9-15.

5. Robert J. Adams, in his discussion of master storyteller Tsune Watanabe, discusses three categories into which the "technical aspect of storytelling may be isolated." (A) Ability to master the technique of storytelling; (B) Ability to conceptualize and fulfill the demands of listeners; and (C) Opportunity to practice storytelling technique in reinforcing situations. Of category "B" Adams says: "in order for a raconteur to be fully recognized in his community as a storyteller, he must understand completely what his listeners expect from him, or in Georges' terms, what the listener's rights are. Conversely, the storyteller must know how to fulfill the listener's expectations, that is, he must know what his duties are and be able to perform them," (p.347). (Robert J. Adams, "Social Identity of a Japanese Storyteller," Ph.D. dissertation, Indiana University, (September, 1972). Adams refers to Robert Georges, "Toward an Understanding of Storytelling Events," *Journal of American Folklore* 82, (Oct-Dec 1969): 313-328).

Robert Georges speaks of the "duties" of the storyteller to the audience. "The storyteller's duties are to formulate, encode, and transmit a message in accordance with socially prescribed rules with which he and the other participants in the storytelling event are familiar." He gives also the duties of the listener and the storyteller's "rights." "The storyteller's rights are that the story receive, decode, and respond to the message in accordance with socially prescribed rules with which he and other participants in the storytelling event are familiar." p. 318. According to Georges, the story *listener's* rights and duties are the converse of the teller's.

6. Robert Georges' discussion of the social identities of storyteller and audience may be useful here. "As the storyteller begins to carry out his duties (as he begins to formulate, encode, and transmit a message), his social identity is relatively more prominent than that of the story listener...As the story listener begins to carry out his duties (as he begins to receive, decode, and respond to the message the storyteller is formulating, encoding, and transmitting), his social identity begins to increase in relative prominence...Once the storyteller begins to receive and decode the responses of the story listener and to interpret and respond to them as feedback, the storyteller and the story listener begin

to shape the message jointly...As the interactions of the storyteller and story listener intensify through their joint participation in the shaping of the message, the message increases in prominence, relatively speaking, and begins to create its own tensions, which reach a peak as the message itself generates maximum interaction between the storyteller and the story listener...As the storytelling event comes to an end, its various aspects become indistinguishable, and the whole storytelling event generates its own unique systems of social and psychological forces that exert pressure on the social environment and upon those whose interactions create that social environment,"
(p. 321-322). Robert A. Georges, "Toward an Understanding of Storytelling Events," *Journal of American Folklore,* 82, No. 326, (Oct-Dec. 1969): 313-328.
7.   Richard   Bauman   suggests   that   a   list   of   "communicative means...serving to key performance" would include "special code; figurative language; parallelism; special paralinguistic features; special formulae; appeal to tradition; disclaimer of performance,"
p. 16. Richard Bauman, *Verbal Art as Performance*, (Prospect Heights, Illinois: Waveland Press, Inc., 1977).
8.   Sandra Silberstein, writing on the difference between male and female courtship stories, suggests that such an "assurance of audience" allows men to speak more slowly and produce more pauses in their speech with "their apparent assumption that a slower delivery with more pauses will not make them vulnerable to interruption--an assumption that seems to be correct." Counting the number of words and fillers per minutes in a series of courtship stories she found that women uttered 166 words per minute average with 8.5 fillers, while men spoke only 125 words with 8.6 fillers. These stories were collected in interviews. Sandra Silberstein, "Gender-based Conventions in Courtship Storytelling," unpublished mss.
9.   Richard Bauman, in his *Verbal Art as Performance*, discusses parallelism   as   one   of   the   communicative   means   for   keying performance. He notes that parallelism is a "fundamental and universal phenomena" and quotes Roman Jakobson's suggestion that parallelism is "the empirical linguistic criterion of the poetic function," (p. 19). Bauman's discussion of Kenneth Burke's views is interesting also here. "Burke has alerted us to the power of formal patterns to elicit the participation of an audience through the arousal of 'an attitude of collaborative expectancy...Once you grasp the trend of the form, it invites participation.' This 'yielding to the formal development,

surrendering to its symmetry as such' (Burke 1969 (1950): 58), fixes the attention of the performer in a relationship of dependence that keeps them caught up in his display," (p. 116). Richard Bauman, *Verbal Art as Performance* (Prospect Heights, Illinois: Waveland Press, Inc., 1977). Bauman is quoting from Kenneth Burke, *A Rhetoric of Motives*, (Berkeley and Los Angeles: University of California Press, 1969); and from Roman Jakobson, "Grammatical Parallelism and Its Russian Facet." *Language* 42, (1966): 399-429.

Jack McConnell, heir to paraphernalia from the
McConnell general store and to its storytelling tradition.

CHAPTER 4
NEW YEAR'S EVE 1985

It is New Year's Eve again. 1985. The party is at Jack and Ledell McConnell's house this year.

The guest list is about the same as last year. Pert and Sally Helt are absent. A new couple has been added to the New Year's Eve group...Tom and Eileen Grizard. Tom and Eileen have lived in Scipio for most of their married life. Tom's parents moved up to Scipio from Kentucky in the 1930's and have become good members of the community. Tom speaks with a soft Kentucky accent and must be a man of mild manner and good humor.

I have talked to Esther, Jack, and Wally by phone and asked them to turn the tape recorder on and let it run all evening. Esther later mails me the tapes for transcription.

The evening arranges itself much like the previous New Year's Eve. After dinner the men settle themselves in the family room. Tonight the TV is on and they fixate on it intermittently between topics of conversation. Tom Grizard and Bill Byford sit to one side and carry on their own quiet conversation throughout much of the evening. Gordon, Wally, Jack, and Nolan watch TV and talk. Their conversation runs from home-repair problems, to fishing trips in Michigan, favorite hounds, and kinds of meat they've eaten...bear, bufalo. It begins to get past everybody's bedtime.

Jack: Don't go to sleep on me, Gordon. You gotta hold up.
Spiv: Tryin' to.

Jack and Ledell have covered the walls of their family room with antiques rescued from the old McConnell store before they sold it. Stored in the attic of the store they found a wealth of the paraphernalia common to the turn of the century country store. Their family room forms a remarkable museum for these items. Spiv points out an old tobacco cutter sitting up on a beam overhead.

Spiv to Wally: That cutter up there.
Wally: Cheese cutter?
Spiv: Nooo. Tobacco cutter.
That used to cut old Star...
Wally: Cut the plugs off?
Spiv: ...for...Lee Bowman.
That's all he chewed was Star.
It was about that thick.
Wally: Yeah, I remember Star had a little metal star poked in it.

The women have been attracted to the conversation. Esther and Margueritte remember that too.

Spiv: Star and Horseshoe. Horseshoe had a little horseshoe...

The women have finished up in the kitchen and joined the men in the family room by this time. The TV has been turned down. The multi-conversations have ceased temporarily to focus on Spiv's remembrances about the tobacco cutter. The moment is ripe for a story. Wally begins and the other men follow in a series of personal anecdote performances.

Wally: Well...
Went down to...Hayden.
When Clyde and I was pretty small.
With Robert and Barney... Sullivan.
Barney was the youngest.
And then Clyde...
And then Robert...
And then me.
There was...four of us...in just...one year.
And uh...that old store down there...
That guy bought...burlap bags.
And you remember the...Twenty Grand...cigarettes?
And the...Wings?
He paid three cents for those burlap bags.
And he'd go there to the back door...
Just throw 'em out there to that...
Had a little shed there and the door was right in
    line with the back door of the store.
He'd buy them burlap bags...and he'd just take 'em
    and throw 'em in that shed.
And them boys'd go back there and get them bags...
Jack: ...get 'em and go back and SELL 'em to him.
Wally: Sell 'em to him AGAIN.
And that's the way they bought their CIGARETTES.

(Spiv is chuckling away)
Wally: SICK...my...GOSH.
Course...we knew we wasn't going to smoke again
    for hard telling when...
And we just lit one right after the other.

Wally: Boy. There was a big guy stayed there at old
man
    Lowes...what was his first name?
Spiv: Jim.
Wally: Jim.
Jack: Oh yeah.
Wally: Down there behind...Margaret Ryan.
And Howard Fleming and this guy got to be pretty good
    buddies.
Well they both SMOKED.
And this was back in the days of the Lucky Strike
    Greens.
This has been a LONG...time ago.

Clyde and I went over there one day.
And we...went from there...to Ettie Thompsons...
    and up through there...just runnin' around.
And we smoked...from the time we left...until we got
    back...
And when I got back...almost to the house...I couldn't
    make it anyfarther.
And I was...DOWN...out there...
Just about where Sam Luellen got down that time in the
    snow.
(Spiv is chuckling)
And...Clyde went on to the house...
And he wanted to know where I was.

He said, "Well he's out there."
Dad come out there...and I was on the ground.
Ooooohhhh I was SICK.
Nnnnnnhhhhh.
He said, "Well..."
Course I suppose I REEKED of tobacco.

And he said, "Well..." he says "You won't DIE."
Spiv: But you'll wish you would.
Wally: But he said, "You'll wish you WOULD."
And he said, "Maybe you'll LEARN something."
Turned around and went back to the HOUSE.
Left...(everyone is laughing already)
Spiv: Left you LAYIN' there.
Wally: Left me LAYIN' there.
(Spiv guffaws)
Wally: And...so help me...
I got just as sick...
the LAST one that I smoked...
as I did the FIRST one.

And I suppose the last one I smoked was...
ten years ago...maybe...
And I thought "Well...you know you're REALLY
gettin' OLD enough...to KNOW..."
Spiv: ...to know better. (laughs)
Wally: ...to know better.
Marybelle: I kept sayin'..."Why do you light 'em UP...
You KNOW they're gonna make you SICK."
Wally shakes his head in disgust and disbelief at
himself:
"Ooohhhh Boyyy."

Tom Grizard has been chatting quietly with Bill Byford much of the evening, not appearing to follow the general conversation. He takes the floor now with his own sick-on-tobacco story. Tom speaks quietly with a soft drawl, which reminds the listener that his folks come from Kentucky. The room gets very quiet when Tom begins his story.

Tom: I know the first time
I ever got sick...was on CIGarettes.
Grandad came.
That...I was over in Kentucky...near Frankfurt.
In what we called the OLD Big Bridge House.
It was a REALLY old house.
Had a slate roof.
Anyway we was ALL gathered over there one Sunday
**   for DINNER.**
So Ledell's dad Cece Shumaker...was there
And he'd just bought a couple of packs of cigarettes...
And laid them up on the TOP of daddy's old Model T
**   CAR.**
And...they all went in there...
Of course the boys all had to WAIT.
That made us MAD. (the audience laughs)
And we swiped Cece's cigarettes...(Bill laughs)
Went around back of the old ice house...
And started puffin' away.
But MAN I'll tell you, I never got so sick in my life...
Ledell: I'll bet you didn't eat any DINNER did you?
Tom: Noooo....
(the women laugh, and Bill Byford offers a story)
Bill: I never did get sick on cigarettes...
But I did on a chew of tobaccer.
I wasn't any bigger...than Warren's little boy...

Dad was a-plowin'...over there in the field
And I went over where the NEIGHBOR was a-plowin'.
And he stopped there...
Just pulled him out a plug of tobacco...
And took a chew of it...
And give it to me.
And I took a chew of it...
Thought I was gettin' along alright.
By God I swallered some of that...
I never got so sick in my LIFE.
(Bill is not a bold storyteller, all have been very quiet
during his story...now they all laugh heartily)

Ledell starts to kid Esther: Well I knew some LADY
    that could chew tobacco and didn't get sick...!
    (the women all laugh...she is obviously referring to
    another story...the women all begin to kid each
    other...)
Esther: (reenacting episode) What'll I do...?
Ledell: I wouldn't have KNOWN what to have done
    with it.
I'm glad you dropped it behind the table...not me.
Woman: I wouldn't have known what to have done with
    it.

With a loud, forceful tone Jack brings the conversation
    back under his control: I got sick on   old...chewin'
    tobacco...and old stub CIGAR.
One that Dad had throwed out there and it rained on it.
Now THAT dude would walk, I'll tell ya.
Bout that long...you know
Right down where she got strong...

Out that back door, you know...and I picked that up,
　　you know, and fired that up...
Maaaan I'm a-tellin' you...
Thought the house on fire!

I stayed with her for a while
And all at once I got dizzy.
(the women are all laughing loudly at Jack)

The other time I got sick on chewin' tobacco.
I mean I was a good big KID.
I was out of school
It was over there 'crost the field from the house over
　　there at the farm.
Tomato patch.
Had tomatoes over there.
Dick Foster.
Course HE always chewed, you know.
And I thought that was really cool...
And I said "GIVE me a chew of that, Dick."
And I had chewed...
off and on some, you know...
before...
But it was awful hot over there...and I must have
　　swallered some of it while I was bendin' over a-
　　pickin'...
Maaan I got sick.
Now THAT boy...
That was my last...
chewin'.

Wally: What was that old man's name that married
    Clary Miller? They lived down there in Uncle
    Earnest's little house...
(Everyone tries to help place this character... they soon
establish that it was Clara Smith...who married Dan
Moreland.)

Wally begins his story:
Well when they got married...
he give out them little...Glenliver,
Do you remember them little bags...?
Clyde and I walked down there...
And we had...probably...like Jack says...
about HALF of one of them.
When we got...were gettin' pretty close to home...
we put it in the old sewer...out there.
We went out the next morning and got that...
and it was dew soaked...
Now I...that didn't BOTHER me...
until we lit 'em up the next mornin'.
(the women are laughing now)
And that smoke...
was as black as COAL smoke.
BUDDY I GOT SICK.
Ledell: (laughing) You was pretty DENSE, wasn't ya?
Wally: It took a long time for me to catch ON.
(the women are all laughing at Wally's predicament)
Spiv: You're as bad as that one. Mary Bailey was
    a-tellin' me about this young couple got married
    and they just kept-a havin' kids...havin' kids...
Just about like THAT you know. (Spiv pounds one
    fist into other palm six times rapidly on "that"
    and Esther breaks out laughing.)

Just as soon as they found out what was A-CAUSIN' it
    they put the STOPS to it!
(The room bursts into loud laughter)
Jack: Wasn't too bad...WAS it.
Nolan: You turned the TAPE off didn't ya, Marybelle?
Marybelle: No. I didn't...
Ledell: Maybe Margaret don't know what CAUSES
    that.
(the laughter continues a while and then dies down)
Jack begins a new story.

Jack: You remember...when Clyde found the cigarette...
Picked the cigarette up along the side of the road
Over there by Clem Balls...?
Along the highway there
He picked it up.
Whole...cigarette.
It had never been smoked or anything.
Come up there.
Some way Dad come around the corner there and
    caught him smokin' it.
He didn't get after him so much for smokin'.
But he asked him where he GOT it.

He said...he picked it up there along the side of the road.
Boy he DID get onto him then.
Pickin' somethin' up at the side of the road there...
    (Anyone could have thrown it out the car
    window...all kinds of people drive up and down the
    highway)

Wally has another story:
We was down there at

the Nettle Creek Bridge one day
And there was a full pack of Chesterfields.
That had never been opened.
And...we walked past it.
And we walked THIS way
And we walked THIS way.
(the women laugh)
And I'll bet you we made fifteen trips past 'em
Before one of us finally... I don't know which one...
Picked it up.
And...just...from that time on.
Why we just...worked on 'em...
pretty GOOD.
(the women laugh and comment about getting sick)

Wally remembers that he saw Howard Fleming the other day at Pat Miller's funeral and talk moves off in a conversational direction leaving the storytelling behind.

This evening four tellers presented six narratives, all on the same topic. In the next chapter we will examine the way these tellers structured their tales for performance.

"That used to cut old star... for Lee Bowman"

CHAPTER 5

HOW TO TELL A STORY IN SCIPIO: STRUCTURING THE PERSONAL NARRATIVE

The narrative text of Scipio's male storytellers follows set patterns. Here Wally Hines, Jack McConnell, Tom Grizard, and Bill Byford tell personal narratives of their first smokes. This storytelling sequence provides a look at a typical session of Scipio conversational storytelling. Each speaker structures his personal narrative in such a way that it becomes humorous anecdote. Their combined style shows us pretty much how to structure a story in Scipio.(1)

To examine the "texts" of these narratives is misleading because these stories were never designed to be "texts." The teller was not *writing* a story in his mind, he was *performing*. The criteria of dramatic art rule here. It is dramatic necessity which controls form, forces tale structure into certain channels, dictates language. And, of course, the *audience* has an "authorship" right in oral tales too. The sensitive teller is constantly shaping his tale to comply with signals sent by his audience. Still, certain interesting things can be said about the dramatic performance as frozen on tape.

THE OPENING SENTENCE: SIGNALING PERFORMANCE

Obviously the first story utterance must signal "this is performance."(2) Otherwise the performer cannot count on capturing the floor and holding it long enough to interest his prospective listeners. Both teller and audience must be well aware of just what signals indicate a launch into performance. Without this knowledge the audience members might talk into a story opening, causing embarrassment for themselves and concern for the teller. The performative markers of voice tone and body language are probably the most important readings to which the audience attends. However, an examination of opening sentences of the stories in this cigarette/tobacco sequence shows that the texts themselves are clearly marked as story openers.(3)

These examples suggest two ways to enter a story into Scipio conversation...either by making a direct topical reference to the conversation just preceding - in this case cigarettes or tobacco - or by beginning with a reference to time past. "When Clyde and I was pretty small", "when they got married", "one day." It would seem that reference to a mythical past time is one key to performance in Scipio.(4) Let's examine openings sentences for first smoke narratives.

Time past references:

Wally: Went down to...Hayden

when Clyde and I was pretty small.
Wally: This has been a LONG...time ago.
Clyde and I went over there one day.
(This story was also prefaced with an audience
query using "there was..." and the formula "This
was back in the days of...")
Jack: You remember...when Clyde found the cigarette...
Wally: We was down there at the Nettle Creek Bridge
one day.

Reference to preceding conversation:

Tom: I know the first time I ever got sick...was on
CIGarettes.
Bill: I never did get sick on cigarettes...but I did on a
chew of tobaccer.
Jack: I got sick on old...chewin' tobacco...and an old
stub CIGAR.
Jack: You remember...when Clyde found the cigarette...

While structuring the first sentence well is crucial in story performance, the story's prefatory matter extends beyond the first performative sentence.

THE STORY PREFACE

Certain bits of prefacing information are traditionally provided for the audience at the beginning of each tale. Sometimes this prefacing data is given in comment before the actual tale commences, at other times the important background information for the tale understanding is given in the tale's opening lines. This raises the question of just where a tale actually begins. The text alone does not always show precisely where a "performance" begins. At times stories may "begin" several times then sidetrack off into added prefacing commentary before the teller finally launches into continuous tale performance.

Wally's story about himself and Clyde getting sick smoking is a good example of this. He opens with a question **"There was a big guy stayed down there at old man Lowes...what was his first name?"** The audience clarifies this for him and Wally continues by recapping just where this fellow lived "Down there behind...Margaret Ryan."

He adds a bit of background information:

And Howard Fleming...and this guy got to be pretty good buddies.
Well, they both smoked.

He sets the stage further:

And this was back in the days of Lucky Strike Greens.
This has been a *long*...time ago.

Then the action begins and continues this time:

Clyde and I went over there one day...

Just where does Wally's "story" actually begin? His question about the "big guy" was obviously pre-story. The information about Howard Fleming seems to be somewhat peripheral to the story which follows, it certainly doesn't have the ring of a story opening. Wally's "And this was back in the days of Lucky Strike Greens. This has been a long...time ago." seems textually like a story opener.

However, Wally's "lucky strike greens" comment was uttered as an aside. Performance probably actually started with his follow-up line "This has been a *long*...time ago." He began to pace his utterance out at this point, stressed the word "long"...paused...and began his story. "Clyde and I..."

Whether it is offered as a pre-story commentary or woven into the opening sentences of the performance itself, there are several functions which the story preface can perform. The story preface can: 1. Show how the teller's topic ties in with previous conversation, 2. Involve the audience through questions, 3. Establish where the tale took place, 4. Establish when the tale took place, and 5. Establish to whom this tale happened.

Tie into conversation

It is polite to tie your story in with the previous topic of conversation. Changing the subject abruptly is a bit egotistical. One should stay on the topic and "follow" the other folks' conversation. The opening statements of the story may take into account the previous tale's topic and include a tie-in to that tale in order to justify the offering of the new tale.(5) As we have noted, this tie-in is often provided by the opening performative sentence.

Wally tells of a first smoke experience. Tom Grizard follows with "the first time *I* ever..." He tells of getting sick. Bill Byford follows with "I never did get sick on cigarettes but I did on..." Jack continues: "*I* got sick on old..." and runs into his second tale..."The other time I got sick on chewin' tobacco..."

Involve the audience through questions

Some tellers, such as Wally, try to elicit audience support for their storytelling effort by asking a question before starting the tale.(6) Others, like Jack and Spiv, usually launch right in and expect everyone to be with them.

In this particular story series, Wally's requests for audience involvement take the form of questions to establish the identity of his characters. "What was that old man's name...?" "There was a big guy stayed down there at old man Lowes...what was his first name?" Jack elicits audience compliance in one story introduction "You remember ...when Clyde found the cigarettes...?"

The involvement of the audience through questions is a useful technique within the narrative too. Wally uses this: "Glenliver...do you remember them little bags?" and again "Remember the Twenty Grand cigarettes? And the Wings?"

Establish where the tale took place

Each teller begins by making clear exactly where action took place. Tom Grizard stresses the exact location of his Kentucky tale, even though naming the "Old Big Bridge House" would mean nothing to the folks in this group. Still, the *setting* is important. Tom adds a bit of description here, perhaps in deference to the fact that Scipio folks are unfamiliar with his home. ("It was a really old house. Had a slate roof.")

Establish when the tale took place

Each teller places his tale in time as well as in space.

Wally: In the days of the Lucky Strike Greens.
Jack: I was a good big kid.
Tom: One Sunday for dinner.
Bill: I wasn't any bigger than Warren's little boy.

As we have seen the first sentence of performance often fulfills this function.

Establish to whom this happened

To Scipio tellers, the "who" of these tales is all important. The story often gets bogged down in problems of clarifying just *who* Clary Smith was. This placing of characters often includes establishing just who they were related to and exactly where they lived. No one ever says, "It doesn't matter. Just get on with the story." Everyone seems to agree that it really *does* matter. These are not just spurious stories told for mere entertainment. This is Scipio history. These stories are interesting because they are relevant. And it is important to get our facts right.

Thus Wally begins the story in this sequence by asking "What was that old man's name that married Clary Miller? They lived down there in Uncle Earnest's little house." It takes considerable group discussion to get these facts straight, but the story doesn't begin until the record is straight.

CONTENT

The tale is stylized through several elements. Let's examine characterization, motivation, conversation, stage direction and description.

Characterization and Motivation:

Scipio tales usually include some motivation. The teller tries to characterize his actors by showing their state of mind.

Wally: ...that...didn't BOTHER me...

until we lit 'em up the next mornin'.

Tom: Oh course the boys all had to WAIT.
That made us MAD.
Bill: And I took a chew of it...
Thought I was gettin' along all right...

Jack: And I thought I was really cool...

Wally: We knew we wasn't going to smoke again for
  hard telling when...

Scipio tellers often give very clear characterization through the tale's action alone.(7) The frame of mind of Wally and his buddies is quite clear in the scene on Devil Creek Bridge. "And...we walked *this* way. And we walked *this* way." As they try to make up their minds to *pick up* the pack of cigarettes found lying on the road.

Dialogue

Only two of these tales use conversation. Jack quotes himself as he asks his tomato picking neighbor "*Give* me a chew of that, Dick." And Wally's father has something to say to *him* about coming home sick and reeking of tobacco. "Well...you won't die...but you'll wish you *would*."

Description

Descriptive passages are practically non-existent in these stories. Tom Grizard stops to describe the Old Big Bridge House down in Kentucky where his story is set. "It was a really old house. Had a slate roof." His use of description here may be triggered by the fact that no one in the group has seen the Old Big Bridge House. Perhaps the *lack* of description in Scipio tales is partially due to the fact that everyone can easily picture just what is being talked about from personal experience.

The only other descriptions in this set of narratives are Wally's comment on the cigar smoke "black as coal smoke." Wally's self descriptor "I reeked of tobacco," and Wally and Jack's functional mention that their cigars were "dew soaked."

Size does receive some descriptive notice in these tales. Wally mentions that his cigar butt was "about that long" and several mention being "small" or "not much bigger than" at the time of the first smoke. These descriptors function mainly as stage directions and time referents though, rather than being used to create images.

Stage Directions

Though descriptive passages are not employed very often in Scipio telling, the use of clear stage direction *is* popular. Wally tells of the Hayden storekeeper throwing out the burlap bags. "he'd go there to the back door...throw 'em out there to that...had a little shed there...that the back door was right in line with the back door of the store." The exact spatial arrangement is important to Wally here.

In another story he tells the audience the exact spot where he fell..."just about where Sam Lewellen got down that time in the snow."

Tom Grizard shows us exactly where Cece's cigarettes were left in his story..."laid them up on *top* of Daddy's old Model T *car*...and...they all went in there...of course the boys all had to *wait*." The boys all wait by the cars while the older folks go into the house for dinner. "...and we swiped Cece's cigarettes...went around the back of the old ice house...and started puffin' away."

Even Jack's brief tale about Clyde smoking the cigarette butt carries full stage directions. "Clyde...picked the cigarette up along the side of the road over there by Clem Balls...along the highway there...Come up there...Dad come around the corner there and caught him smokin' it." The audience understands "come up there" to refer to the McConnell store corner.

Ac`ion

Scipio tales rely heavily on action to get their message across. Characterization is shown through the character's *actions*. In addition to giving clear stage directions for just where everyone stood, the story tells us precisely how everyone moved. Bill Byford tells of his first chew.
"And I went over where the neighbor was a-plowin'. And he stopped there...just pulled him out a plug of tobacco...and took a chew of it...and give it to me. And I took a chew of it..."

We find that characterization, motivation, conversation, stage direction, and action are the main tools of the Scipio storyteller, with description playing a minor part. The Scipio teller is praised for his ability to "put in all the details," but those details refer to a picture of action and thought, not a descriptive image of objects.

STYLE IN THE TALE TEXT

Confident, unhesitating speech

The skill of these Scipio tellers is apparent in the self confident way in which each narrates his tale. The entire tale telling sequence included only one "uh", three "you knows" and four minor restarts. The tales proceed logically and coherently from start to finish.(8) Even the shyest of the tellers, Bill Byford, tells with perfect mastery of the form when he does tell.

The teller's fast moving, clearly outlined tales make it "easy on the listener." Their coherency is not achieved through perfectly structured sentences, rather it relies on frequent interjection and constant sentence truncation.

Truncated sentences

The truncated sentence is used skillfully to add emphasis and to pace the story. Jack begins his story of Clyde smoking the cigarette butt with a long rambling question "You remember...when Clyde found the cigarette...picked the cigarette up along the side of the road over there by Clem Balls...? Along the highway there..." (Suddenly he gains momentum and begins to stylize his speech.)

He picked it up.
Whole...cigarette.
It had never been smoked or anything.
Come up here...

The pacing shows clearly that Jack is in the midst of "storyifying."

Of the 97 sentences spoken in these narratives, 13 were structurally truncated, that is they lacked either a subject or a verb or both. This doesn't tell the whole story, however, for many more sentences, in fact most, were truncated in delivery. For example, the sentence "Barney was the youngest, and then Clyde, and then Robert, and then me" was spoken as four distinct utterances.

"Barney was the youngest
And then Clyde.
And then Robert.
And then me."

Parallel Structure

These truncated sentence fragments often begin to cluster together in parallel arrangements, creating an almost poetic effect for the listener.

Bill Byford: "And he stopped there...
Just pulled him out a plug of tobacco...
And took a chew of it...
And give it to me.
And I took a chew of it..."

Thought I was gettin' along alright.
By God I swallered some of that...
I never got so sick in my LIFE.

Or Wally, from another tale:
And...we walked past it.
And we walked THIS way,
And we walked THIS way.
And I'll bet we made fifteen trips past 'em
Before one of us finally...
I don't know which one...
Picked it up.

Because the effect of delivery style on text is so strong, I discuss stylistic elements of the text, such as parallelism, also in the chapter on tale delivery.

Colorful language:

The Scipio teller enlivens his talk with colorful phrases... phrases which surprise and delight the listener. Such phrases must be drawn from within the idiom of the Scipio folk group in which they are used, or they must be constructed artfully enough to sound as if they belong. And they must be used infrequently enough to still surprise the ear and bring instant delight.

Instances of such colorful speech from our first smoke stories might include Wally's poetic "back in the days of the Lucky Strike Greens..." And Jack's "Now *that* dude would *walk*, I'll tell ya," and his "Thought the house was on fire!"

The group's repeated references to brands from the olden days functioned as "colorful" references as well-- "Glenliver," "Chesterfields," "Model T," and those "Lucky Strike Greens" --all evoked the surprise and delight of sudden memory.

Alliteration

Alliteration appears infrequently in Scipio narratives and when it does appear it seems to be a function of performance. It pops into speech because it feels good and sounds good. One example was Jack's "Beg, borry, or steal" from the 1984 party.

Simile

In a narrative style with little use for descriptive passages, the use of simile is not strong. Still an occasional simile does appear as in Wally's cigar smoke "as black as coal smoke."

Allusion

The reference to other stories within a story occurs often in Scipio telling. Folks possess a common fund of tales. Any really good story gets told several times. Since many folks in the group are familiar with a whole body of lore about the characters in the area, Wally can make an internal reference such as "that's the same place where Sam Luellen got down in the snow" without stopping to explain.

Formula

Wally seems to be the only other teller in this session who relies on formula in his tales' openings and closings.(9) "One day..." "from that time on..." "this has been a *long*...time ago..." and in ending, "And that's the way we..."

The use of formulaic expressions within the tale is common however. Examples: Wally's "You're really getting old enough to know better," "We just lit one right after the other," "You won't die, but you'll wish you would." And both Tom and Bill: "I never got so sick in my life."

The use of formulaic expressions facilitates the tale jumping from the audience. Spiv successfully jumped Wally's line:

"You won't die..."
Spiv: "But you'll wish you would."
Wally (agreeing): "...but you'll wish you would."

Wally might or might not have meant to say that, but aesthetics required that he keep the pattern established by Spiv's line ending.

Internal Laugh Lines

The best tales are often marked by the use of internal laugh lines. Jack is a master at this use of the repeated laugh line throughout his telling. (His tellings on New Year's Eve 1984 have several examples of this.) He gets an internal laugh with "Maaan, I'm a-tellin' you...Thought the house was on fire!" In his cigar stub story, Wally achieves an internal laugh with his "Walked *this* way...walked *this* way..." in his tale of picking up the cigarettes from the bridge. And Tom Grizard gets a good laugh with his mid-tale comment "Of course us boys had to *wait*, That made us *mad*." Obviously, it is the delivery as much as the content that is bringing down the house in these mid-joke laugh lines.

ENDING: PUNCH LINE OR TALE ENDING

Each narrative ends with a short stressed statement, designed to evoke a laugh. Since there is no "punch" line to these stories, the claim of just how sick one got can serve that function.(10)

Wally: And that smoke
was as black as coal smoke.
BUDDY I GOT SICK.

Tom Grizard: But MAAAN, I'll tell you...
I never got so sick in my entire LIFE...

Jack: MAAAN I got sick.
Now that...boy...
That was my last...
Chewin'.

**Wally again: Turned around and went back to the
    HOUSE.**
Left me LAYIN' there.

Wally has a story which does not end in nausea. He
closes his narrative with a formulaic ending and a capping
phrase:

And...just...from that time on...
why we just...worked on 'em...
pretty GOOD.

The Scipio humorous anecdote, following the joke format
prefers to end with a punch line. In the absence of an actual
joke line, the last line can be punched up by shortening,
pacing, and forceful delivery to lend it a comic force
worthy of any tale's end.(11, 12)

TALE CAPPING

Though the tale itself can be said to end with its punch
line or tale ending, we saw in our discussion of the 1984
party that the tale is far from over at this point.(13) The
audience must be given a chance to laugh, comment, poke
fun at the teller. And the teller must continue his own
vocalizations with repetition of the tale's punch line, replies
to his tormentors, or other humorous asides. These capping
phrases should be brief, probably philosophical, and/or
humorous.

After Wally's sick-in-the-yard smoking tale, he adds
"And I suppose the last one I smoked was...ten years
ago...maybe."...and I thought 'Well...you know, you're

really gettin' *old* enough...to *know*..." Spiv completes it for him..."to know better." Wally: "...to know better."

At times the teller may extend these capping comments and bridge into a next tale. They can, in other words, be a way of holding the floor.

Wally follows his story of selling burlap bags with "SICK, my *gosh*!" "Course we knew we wasn't going to smoke again for hard telling when...And we just lit one right after the other." He pauses a moment and begins another tale. "There was a big guy stayed down there at old man Lowe's..."

SUMMARY

Let's look then at what we've discovered about the Scipio tale text.

1. The first sentence signals performance
   -through textual reference
   -through reference to time past
2. The story preface:
   -ties in with previous conversation
   -involves the audience through questions
   -establishes where the tale took place
   -establishes when the tale took place
   -establishes to whom the tale happened
3. The tale content is expressed through
   -characterization
   -motivation
   -dialogue
   -description
   -stage direction
   -action
4. Style in the text is achieved through
   -confident, unhesitating speech
   -truncated sentences
   -parallel structure
   -colorful language
   -alliteration
   -metaphor
   -allusion
   -formulae
5. Internal laugh lines release tension in mid-tale.
6. The ending is marked by
   -a punch line or a clearly crafted tale ending

-tale capping which extends beyond the "last line" of the tale.

We have talked about style in text and performance and discussed the audience's role in the storytelling event. There is another interesting question to ask of Scipio's storytelling: "What does it DO for Scipio?" The next chapter will give one possible answer.

NOTES:
CHAPTER 5

1.   For useful discussion of the structure of personal narrative, see William Labov and Joshua Waletzky, "Narrative Analysis: Oral Versions of Personal Experience" in *Essays on the Verbal and Visual Arts*, June Helm, editor(A.M.S. press, 1988).

2.   See Richard Bauman's chapter on "The Keying of Performance" in *Verbal Art as Performance* (Prospect Heights, Illinois: Waveland Press, Inc., c. 1977, 1984), pp. 15-24.

3.   Margaret L. McLaughlin in *Conversation: How Talk is Organized* discusses the various ways in which a conversational story may be introduced into conversation. The initiating turn could contain a number of different speech acts, including offer, characterizations, stage-setting, admonitions, and so forth. "The preface section often proposes some initial characterization of the event...A third function of the preface sequence is to make some reference to the time or occasion when the event to be recounted took place...Other functions of the preface sequence include attributing a forthcoming narrative or joke to a third party, and admonishing the recipient not to repeat the story." Margaret L. McLaughlin, *Conversation: How Talk is Organized.* (Beverly Hills: Sage Publications, 1984), pp. 186-189.

4.   William Hugh Janson, writing of similar tale material defines his tales as "set in the Golden Age that the teller knew or had heard of in his youth...Such a time setting gives them a faint fictional aura despite the fact that they involve real persons doing real things in a real place." William Hugh Janson, "Purpose and Function in Modern Local

Legends of Kentucky: in *Varia Folklorica*, Alan Dundes, editor. (The Hague: Mouton, 1978), pp. 123-143.

5. Margaret L. McLaughlin gives a good review of the literature on story sequencing devices in her *Conversation: How Talk is Organized*, (Beverly Hills: Sage Publications, 1984). She lists eight story sequencing devices: 1. explicit repeat of a significance statement, 2. implicit repeat of a significance statement, which connects one's story to prior tellers, 3. supportive story prefixed phrases such as "yeah, that's true, one time I...", 4. topping, "You think that's bad, wait'll you hear this one!" 5. reinterpretation, retelling another way, 6. disjunct markers "Not to change the topic but...", 7. embedded repetitions, in which a triggering element in a prior recounting is repeated but not marked, and 8. marked repeats which explicitly cite the element that is a participant in both recountings. (p. 193)

6. Margaret L. McLaughlin (ibid) in her discussion of conversational storytelling suggests that "The preface sequence minimally consists of two turns, one by the potential storyteller and one by her intended recipient." However, McLaughlin's two-turn preface to conversational storytelling does not always apply to the Scipio humorous anecdote. The more confident tellers after begin without bothering to solicit a request for telling from the audience. The "initiating turn" runs right into the story itself, audience compliance is given by their attentive body language, and perhaps a few back-channel vocalizations. One mark of the "performed" anecdote may be that it takes precedence over usual rules of conversational turn.

7. Olrik's "Epic Laws of Folk Narrative" mentions "the general principle that each attribute of a person and thing must be expressed in actions--otherwise it is nothing...If one were to begin "There was once a young motherless girl who was unhappy but beautiful and kind..." it would be entirely too complicated a thought for a Marchen. It is much better when these ideas are expressed in action and when these actions are all connected." Axel Olrik, "Epic Laws of Folk Narration" in Alan Dundes, *The Study of Folklore*. (Englewood Cliffs, N.J.: Prentice-Hall, 1965), p. 137.

8. John McDowell suggests the audience of informal narrative holds its narrators accountable on two scores: narratives have to be both coherent and entertaining. John McDowell, "Coherency and Delight: Dual Canons of Excellence in Informal Narrative," *Folklore Forum Bibliographic and Special Series*, No. 12, (1974): 97-106.

McDowell discusses the problems of the speaker in thinking on his feet to formulate coherent sentences. "Normal syntactic relations are skewed through three aberrant processes: 1. incorrect ordering of phrases, 2. mismatching of phrases, 3. omission of implied phrases." The speakers "simply find the pace too demanding to allow for the complete specification of syntactic relationships. And...he is continually plagued with fragments left behind in the process of sentence retracking." (p. 100).

McDowell points out the audience's role in "making sense" out of the speaker's story. "One possible explanation of the audience's tolerance of ill-formed sentences is that the communication of personal narratives is a reciprocal affair. The narrator encodes his anecdote to the best of his ability, under the circumstance. The audience then actively decodes the narrator's utterances, in a creative manner aimed at reconstructing the probable syntactic shell the narrator had in mind. Assuming that the audience contributed in this way, the narrator enjoys a greater latitude of syntactic license, without which sustained spontaneous speech might be impossible," (p. 101).

McDowell talks also of the use of fillers to stall for time while thinking. The speech setting he was studying was characterized by

1) casual interaction, calling for informal speech style, 2) limited amount of time in which to formulate utterance, and 3) intense competition for the floor, calling for steady production of utterances.

9.   Robert J. Adams compared his Japanese teller Tsune Watanabe with Slavic storyteller Mrs. Vinokurova, who was studied by Azadovski. He found that both neglected to use the elaborate opening formula available in their cultures. Instead, each "either names the characters; states immediately what the characters were doing; or names the characters and gives the place where the action begins." (p. 308) Adams suggests that the use of such straight-to-the-point openings may be more usual than printed folktale texts suggest. "...judging from my experience with other Japanese storytellers, the use of such formulas is not as pervasive as is indicated by texts which have been published. Some collectors insist that the storyteller not forget to begin with a formulaic opening, so after being reminded a few times, the expected formula is invariably given and the collector is satisfied that he is getting the genuine tradition," (p. 304). Robert J. Adams, "The Social Identity of a Japanese Storyteller," (Ph.D. diss., Indiana University, September 1972).

10. William Hugh Janson, speaking of Kentuckian local legends, notes a brevity of endings which is also typical of Scipio tales. "Of these forty-one tales...thirty lead up to--and abruptly stop with what some particular person said in a specific situation. The other eleven all exist to tell what a particular person did at a specific moment; having exposed that action, they promptly cease," (p. 124). William Hugh Janson, "Purpose and Function in Modern Local Legends of Kentucky" in Alan Dundes, ed. *Varia Folkorica*, (The Hague: Mouton, 1978), pp. 123-143.

11. Robert Adams studied a Morgan County, Indiana raconteur with similar tale capping habits. Adams comments on the function of these "postscripts" within conversation. "Sullivan has a habit of making some type of closing comment about nearly every story he tells. These comments form a sort of postscript to the jokes and help to integrate them into the flow of conversation. The post-joke comment may be the pointing out of, and application of the moral of the story; a commentary on some salient point; a repetition of the punch line; or an observation on the reaction of a past or future audience. He is rarely content to tell a joke and let it stand unadorned. Rather, he adds the comment to make a transition from the joke itself to the everyday world." Robert J. Adams, "Raconteur and Repertoire: A Study of a Southern Indiana Storyteller and His Material." (Bloomington, Indiana University, Master's Thesis, July 1966), p. 42.

12. Olrik's "Epic Laws of Folk Narrative" cites the "Law of Opening" and the "Law of Closing." "The Sage begins by moving from calm to excitement and after the concluding event, in which a principal character frequently has a catastrophe, the Sage ends by moving from excitement to calm...The constant reappearance of this element of terminal calm shows that it is based, not just on a manifestation of the inclination of an individual narrator, but on the formal constraints of an epic law," (p. 132). Axel Olrik, "Epic Laws of Folk Narrative" in Alan Dundes, *The Study of Folklore*. (Englewood Cliffs, N.J.: Prentice-Hall, 1965). Since the Scipio humorous anecdote usually ends abruptly with a sudden funny action or saying, the tag lines and repeated endings may function to restore gradually the "terminal calm" of which Olrik speaks.

13. Discussing the closing sequence of a conversational story, McLaughlin (*Conversation*, p. 191-192) notes that it "may be signaled in a variety of ways, including gist or upshot formulations as well as other story-exit devices...Formulations...often serve to terminate topical

talk generally, and they do the same work in the case of stories, furthermore...a formulation in a story closing sequence may very well serve the additional function of displaying the point of the story from the teller's perspective...A further function of closing sequence formulations is to demonstrate for the recipient the implication of the story for subsequent talk...The recipient is then expected to demonstrate how the story will inform her own succeeding remarks,". Because of the way in which Scipio's humorous anecdotes are skillfully woven into the general conversation, McLaughlin's comments on conversation seem useful. Some of the functions of her "closing sequence" may be carried out in the Scipio humorous anecdote by the tale's capping sequence.

CHAPTER 6
SELF-TALK IN SCIPIO: THE EFFECT OF NARRATIVE FORM ON WORLD VIEW

I have mentioned that the humorous anecdote is the favored form of storytelling in Scipio. Tales of tragedy and despair are not popular. When it is necessary to convey news of tragic affairs this is done in hushed tones, conversationally, without the structure of "story." If it is at all possible to find humor in any tragedy, this is done. The group obviously wants to feel optimistic, to see a ray of sunshine in every cloud, and to always look on the funny side of every story. Folks here are hard working, tough. They expect a certain amount of pain in every life and are prepared to "grin and bear it." Sayings such as "It'll all come out in the wash" and "It was all for the best" are popular. In Scipio storytelling broken zippers and green-at-the-gills cigar smoking become events to remember with laughter. We can see that this storytelling reflects Scipio's world view(1), but does it also *affect* world view?(2)

In Scipio the humorous anecdote is a popular narrative form. Folks get in the habit of retelling the day's mishaps in the form of a humorous tale of misadventure.(3)

It seems likely that people "talk to themselves" in the same narrative patterns which they are accustomed to using. Jack McConnell's balky umbrella story told during the 1984 New Year's party is a good example of the personal mishap as humorous anecdote. And internal evidence in the story suggests that Jack was seeing this as a funny episode even as it occurred. Let's take a closer look at Jack's umbrella narrative.

Jack: So THEN.
On the umbrella.
She gave me a new UMBRELLA for Christmas one
time.
Never had used it.
It was one of them you just flip a button you know
and boy (slaps hands) she'd go right up and
boy it was really HANDY...
Pulled her back down. (illustrates)
So I had that up in Indianapolis.
And we was goin' up there on Pennsylvania Street to a
restaurant.
Man just a-pourin' down rain.
And I got up there and went to pull that umbrella down
and she wouldn't come DOWN.
She was locked open.
Well you couldn't leave it on Pennsylvania Street cause
it was gonna blow away, or somebody'd STEAL it.

So there I was...
Well...when I was tryin' to pull that down
Candid Camera had gone off the air, but I thought it'd
come back on because I looked around for
somebody to be...

some news reporter to be takin' my PICTURE tryin'
    to get that down.
And I told the boys...I said "Well go in there and get us
    a table. I'll take this back to the City-County
    Building."
So it was two blocks...
back to the City-County Building.
Couldn't get it through the revolving door part cause
    it was still open, see.

There was another door you go in.
Well I tried to get through THAT door.
The door was about that wide (Jack gestures)...and that
    old umbrella was about THAT wide, see.
I STILL couldn't work her around.
And I finally worked around and got in there
    I was inside that building walkin' along there
    with that umbrella up you know...

Everybody lookin' at me...and I went down to the
    garage...
    where the CAR was parked.

And I thought...
"Well I can't get her YET"
So I just took her like THAT you know (illustrates)...
And I just BROKE ever one of them things...
And I just folded her up and laid her in the trunk.

Jack must have been hungry, wet, and frustrated. He
was using up his lunch hour wrestling with a balky
umbrella rather than enjoying the company of his friends at
the restaurant. This can't have been a very pleasant

experience for Jack. And yet to hear him tell it...it sounds like the funniest thing in the world. Jack's reference to his thought about Candid Camera suggests that even as the episode was going on Jack was seeing it through the storyteller's eyes...seeing the funny part of it. He may well have been formulating this story for retelling as a humorous anecdote even while he was in the midst of the frustration. Certainly he would have had the anecdote whipped into shape for telling by the time he got back to the restaurant, wet, bedraggled, out-of-breath...but with a tale of woe they wouldn't believe...one that would have them doubled over with laughter.

In Jack's circle of friends the humorous anecdote is a prime ingredient of conversation. Everyone has his store of funny stories to tell. The day's events are restructured into humorous anecdote format suitable for sharing. You might as well laugh at your troubles...you can't do anything *about* them.

But what if Jack had belonged to a different group of friends? We have all encountered groups in which gloom and doom form the major topics of conversation. Groups in which the members dwell on the horrors of their last operation, the terminal illness of so and so's friend, or the disaster which struck Emma Biddle's niece. If Jack had belonged to such a group, would his framing of his own story have been different? Would it still have induced humor...or would it have been played out for sympathy...as one of life's many disasters to be borne in misery?

If Jack had retold his umbrella misadventure as a tale of woe rather than as "funny story," would not this self-telling have *affected* as well as reflected the way he felt about the episode? It seems that the form of personal narrative prevalent in one's mini-culture may affect the way one perceives reality.(4)

The disaster-as-humorous-anecdote is a major form of communication among Jack McConnell's friends in Scipio. During that same New Year's evening, Nolan Spencer told the funny story about the time his dog ate up the Christmas ham; Jack and his wife Ledell told about the time the gas pedal stuck on her car and she kept driving around and around the block calling for help; and I told about the time the mole tunneled under our house causing my husband, in his efforts to gas or drown the mole, to first flood the basement, and then fill the house with poison gas. As I recall, he didn't *appear* to find that terribly amusing at the time.

Master tellers, such as Jack McConnell, probably get the most mileage out of their funny stories. They actively seek out audiences to which they can tell their stories, and will repeat the newly-formed tale several times to different groups. Jack's umbrella tale has provided a source of considerable entertainment for his Scipio friends. When he began to tell it to a new listener (me) on New Year's Eve, everyone at the party closed ranks excitedly and settled down amid a flurry of teasing comments to hear "Jack's umbrella story" again.

And, of course, these stories can only get *better* with each telling. The master teller is known for his ability to improve on his stories as he goes along. Nolan Spencer told us the funny story of how his dog ate up part of their ham when they set it out to cool. Then he added, "When I told it at work I made it *worse*. I told he got it *all*!" The storyteller just sort of gets in the habit of "making his tale *worse*." The more he tells it...the funnier it gets. After a while, the original episode may begin to look mild by comparison.

The master teller has such an eye for the humorous in events that sometimes he can't resist imagining an even funnier ending which his story could have had. Spiv tells the story of catching a big catfish in a hollow log. At one point in the story, Spiv has reached his arm way down into a hole on top of this submerged hollow log and is trying to entice out a big catfish lying there. Bill Byford is poised at the other end of the log with a net over the hole, ready to catch the fish if it bolts. Spiv gets tickled while recounting the story and adds an aside:

> **And the funny part of it...**
> **I just couldn't keep from thinkin'...**
> **If that fish went out of there...**
> **And Bill kindy overbalanced a little bit...**
> **Sittin' there holdin' the net like that...**
> **He'd just take Bill right off the back END.**

That didn't happen, of course, Spiv *got* the fish and the story had a different ending. But he just couldn't help thinking...what if...

Perhaps the raconteur whose narrative sense lets him see at a glance that "It could have been worse..." is already on the road to feeling a little better about his disastrous experience. In the actual ending of the fish-in-the-log story, Spiv's hand got mauled and his bait bucket torn to shreds...still "It could have been worse..." Bill might have fallen into the river. Of course, if he *had*...that would have been *really* funny.

Even old age and infirmity are treated with humor in Scipio. One afternoon Spiv and I walked through the Catholic cemetery near his house looking at the old gravestones. When we returned, Esther questioned him about the expedition. Together they turn a perfectly disastrous situation into a humorous anecdote.

Spiv: I couldn't see to read 'em...
And she'd read 'em and I couldn't hear her...
Esther: And then you couldn't *remember*...
if you *did* hear her!
Spiv: Now ain't that a *sight*!

They both laugh at the infirmities of old age, companionably.

Their ability to turn their reality into a pleasingly parallel verbal play makes it all seem more bearable.

Spiv Helt and Jack McConnell are two of Scipio's *master* tellers. But it is not only the master teller who makes a funny story of his misadventures. Many members of the group use this technique for retelling their misfortune tales to themselves. The reticent individual, who performs seldom, may be retelling the story to *himself* in his group's narrative style. Or he may tell his story quietly to only one close friend in an intimate setting, with few performance markers. The tale still functions as a means of defining reality.(5)

Sometimes an informant will preface a particular narrative with "I never told this to anyone before." It seems certain, however, that the teller retold the narrative to *himself.* If it is a particularly meaningful narrative, it probably has been retold many times and can be assumed to have shaped itself, though *without* the added shaping force of an audience other than oneself.

Telling to *oneself* (or self talk) must be seen as telling to an audience of one. But a very critical audience of one. The tale is shaped, turned over, and modified with each telling. The tale will be molded to meet one's emotional needs, one's need to make sense out of the story...to make things come out in a way which is consistent with one's own view of the world. The tale will be modified also to fit the notions of verbal aesthetics which one holds. The story will be retold with increasing stylistic polish and its "literary" form will be refined with repeated self tellings.

We can see that an individual's ability to deal with adversity is determined in part by the self-talk prototypes available to him. The scripts for telling ourselves how we feel are learned. However, individuals may be selective in choosing the scripts for their own repertoire of self-talk. Approved patterns will vary from group to group, and may change over time within one group. An individual may belong to more than one storytalking in-group. A narrator may formulate varying versions of his adventure to meet the norms of different speech communities, and an individual may select to belong to in-groups which favor the type of story scripting he feels most comfortable with. But whether one belongs to an in-group by choice or by chance, the preferred form of one's mini-culture may affect the way one views reality.(6)

The individual raised in a culture which favors the humorous anecdote as a set way to retell life's little misfortunes will likely have a happier outlook on life because of this. Scipio's proclivity for the humorous narrative *affects* as well as reflects the world view of the folks who live there. Life *is* the way it *is*. You might as well *laugh*.

NOTES
CHAPTER 6

1. Studies which demonstrate this include: Juha Pentikainen, *Oral Repertoire and World View: An Anthropological Study of Marina Takalo's Life History.* FF Communications No. 219 (Helsinki: Suomalainen Tiedeakatemia Academia Scientiarum Fennica, 1978); Henry Glassie, *Passing the Time in Ballymenone: Culture and History of an Ulster Community.* (Philadelphia: University of Pennsylvania Press, 1982) and Alessandro Falassi, *Folklore by the Fireside: Text and Context of the Tuscan Veglia.* (Austin: University of Texas, 1980). For a useful discussion and extensive reading suggestions on the topic of world view see Barre Toelken, *The Dynamics of Folklore*, (Boston: Houghton Mifflin, 1979), Chapter 25.

2. Whorf has commented on the question of which came first, language patterns or the cultural norms which they reflect. He concludes that "In the main they have grown up together, constantly influencing each other. But in this partnership the nature of language is the factor that limits free plasticity and rigidifies channels of development in the more autocratic way." (p. 156) Benjamin Lee Whorf. *Language, Thought and Reality: Selected Writings of Benjamin Lee Whorf.* Ed. John B. Carroll. (New York: The Technology Press of Massachusetts Institute of Technology and John Wiley & Sons, Inc. 1956).

3. Linda Degh says of her Hungarian informant from the Gary-East Chicago Region, Steve Boda: "Uncle Steve was a carefree, happy-go-lucky man who liked his work, his food and his booze, and resolved his problems in life by a strong sense of humor. Whatever happened to him, no matter how disadvantageous it looked, he made it appear funny," (p. 109). Linda Degh, "Symbiosis of Joke and Legend: A Case of Conversational Folklore" in *Folklore Today: A Festchrift for Richard M. Dorson.* Edited by Linda Degh, Henry Glassie, Felix J. Oinas. (Bloomington: Indiana University, 1976), pp. 101-122. This attitude is a common one among storytellers, probably because it is the out-going optimistically happy fellow whose stories please his audiences most, who is encouraged to tell most, who becomes the best storyteller, and who is collected by the folklorist.

4. Linda Degh, writing of the Canadian-Hungarian Janos Huszar and his wife says, "Both of them are high strung and sensitive with a strong

affinity to the gloomy side of life." "Their interesting and well elaborated stories serve the purpose of showing the negative side of life. None of them offers consolation. Within the frame of the life history, the single episodes function as exempla destined to show the tragedy of their life," (p. 221). Linda Degh, *People in the Tobacco Belt: Four Lives*. Canadian Centre for Folk Culture Studies Paper No. 13, (Ottawa: National Museums of Canada, 1975).

5.   Bauman, Richard, "The La Have Island General Store: Sociability and Verbal Art in a Nova Scotia Community" JAF 85 n. 338 (Oct-Dec 1972): 330-343. "It is clear from the nature of the genre that yarns were a means of organizing personal experience for a presentation to others...Much of what the Island men did, they did alone or away from their home community---consequently much of what the men felt to be important about themselves could only be imparted to others by telling them about it. By the same token, these were the kinds of things each man wanted to know about others," (p. 336).

6.   Rosemary O. Joyce seems also to suggest that narrative form reflects world view. Of her "consultant" Sarah Flynn Penfield (pseud.), she writes "...there is a grim, pessimistic, gloom-and-doom theme in Sarah's conversations that belies her brisk, positive, jovial demeanor. This may simply be an outgrowth of her somewhat recent involvement with a specialized religious sect, and a reflection of the normative for that group," (p. 47). Rosemary O. Joyce: *A Woman's Place: The Life History of a Rural Grandmother*. (Columbus: Ohio State University, 1983).

*   *   *

Well, New Year's Eve in Scipio is over and we've about worried those poor stories to death. Text, performance, audience, function, that was a lot to bite off. You can pack up and go on home now if you like. Or you can stick around and go over to Spiv Helt's with me for a while and we'll see what HE has to say.

PART II

SPIV HELT, MASTER STORYTELLER

SPIV HELT: MASTER STORYTELLER

Spiv Helt is Scipio's acknowledged master storyteller. When I asked Jeanette down at the store about local storytellers, she told me, "You'd better talk to Spiv Helt up here. He's the one that can really tell them." Spiv has a lot of stories to tell. Most folks like to start him off on the old codgers who used to live around Scipio, or the antics that went on at McConnell's and Milholland's stores back in the old days. And, of course, Spiv would always be good for a fish story.

Let's visit with Spiv for a spell and hear some of his stories. Spiv's wife Esther will be around during most of the tellings. His brother Pert and wife Sally will be there off and on. And Spiv's old fishing buddy Wally Hines may drop in.

As we listen we'll think about just what these particular stories may be doing for the community. Do they fill some special Scipio need? And, of course, we'll take a closer look at Spiv's storytelling style later to see just what it is that makes Spiv Helt the one who can "really tell them."

CHAPTER 7
OLD CODGERS: STORY AS CAUTIONARY TALE.

In order to learn how to get along in a group, it helps to find out just what sorts of behavior are not acceptable. What kind of behavior leads to gossip? What kind of behavior is laughable? The group's stories teach these things. They are a way of saying without *saying*. By listening we learn without having to be *told* just what behavior is appropriate.

The community is not tolerant of individuals who are too gullible, folks who take themselves too seriously, or those who are always looking for a little praise or reassurance. And of course to fit in, one must be able to take a joke. Those individuals who miss the mark are the easy butt of community joking. Spiv's stories clearly show the community attitude toward the "old codger" and the "oddity."

Though these tales are told because they are funny stories, they function well as cautionary tales, reminding

the listeners that certain kinds of behavior are laughable, to
be avoided lest one risk becoming an "oddity" oneself.

*   *   *

One hot July evening Spiv's brother Pert and wife Sally
come to visit. We all sit out back catching whatever breeze
there is. I have my tape recorder turned on and am trying to
get Spiv to tell some of his stories. It doesn't take much to
get him going. Pert nods along as the perfect encourager to
Spiv's tales. The women fade in and out of the
conversation. They become interested in one of Spiv's
tales...then suddenly remember a bit of gossip they forgot
to tell each other and start up their own conversation for a
while.

Spiv's house sits on a hillside overlooking Scipio. As he
talks he gestures toward the spot below where lightning
struck the locust tree. He points to the road leading to Old
Bill Little's house. Below us the country store, the garage,
the church are all laid out on the main drag through town.
The setting for his stories lies before us as he tells.

**Sally: Well, Spiv, I've got one I always get a kick out of.
It was Uncle Ernest and that fellow that went to sit up
     with the...(1)**
Spiv: Bill LITTLE.
Pert: Oooh. Look OUT!
Spiv laughs: Old Bill Little.
This is a true story.
He lived down there in the country and his wife died.
**Well Bill and...you don't know Wiggle Emily. But
     Wiggle...**
**He's seventy-seven years old now. And he was a
     PISTOL.**

He'd devil you or somebody...REGARDLESS.

And back THEN they didn't take the corpse to the
funeral home.

They left them at the house.

And they'd always...two or three of the neighbors come
in and sit with them...all night...'cept the CATS.

Had to watch the cats and the rats because that was the
first thing they thought about when anybody died
was jumping right on there and gettin' 'em a MESS,
you know.

(Spiv laughs as Margaret gasps in horror)

And old Bill...he was an oddity.

And he had about six or eight cats.

Big old cats.

And they jist swarmed around the back door.

Everytime he went out...there them cats was.

And they was a-sittin' there you know...thinkin' of
something to talk about...and pass the time away in
the evening and Wiggle...he happened to think...

He set there along the wall with a straight-backed chair
and he jist leaned back against the wall...

He'd reach back there against the wall...it was
paper...paper wall paper...and he'd...(Spiv makes a
scratching noise underneath his chair)...

And Bill'd grab the broom. And he'd run out and he'd
KNOCK CATS! (Spiv laughs)

'Bout five minutes and then he'd come back and he'd
cuss 'em out and go on.

And then he'd come back and sit down.

And Wiggle'd jest let him get sit down good till he'd
(Spiv scratches under the chair again, laughs)...
Scratch again.

He said that went on till after midnight.
Wiggle finally quit.
He said the old man never did catch on what it was.
He'd grab that broom ever time and go out and BAT
    CATS.(2)
Margaret: Oh that's TERRIBLE. (laughing)
Pert: Knock the CATS away.
Spiv: He said, "they ALWAYS do that," he said...
"Ever time somebody dies they ALWAYS do that!"
Uncle Earnest was settin' up with...
Uncle Earnest knew well enough what was goin' on, you
    know...
He'd have to laugh regardless.(3)

But they had a lotta fun out of Old Bill Little.(4)

One story generally leads to another.

Herschel Webster told me one time
(Spiv uses a weak, hoarse voice imitating Herschel
    Webster)
He says, "Bill comes in here..." he says
"Bill comes in here and borrows ten dollars from me"
And he said, "he don't no more need that ten dollars
    than I need a wooden leg."
He said..."He just wants to see if his credit's good"
(Spiv laughs).
He says, "I'll loan him ten and sometimes it won't be an
    hour till he'll be back with it.
And the next time may be two or three days...but he
    always comes back with it."
Says, "I always loan it to him"
Says, "Always wants a ten."

Says, (under his breath) "He just wants to see if his
   CREDIT'S good."

Spiv: I went to a sale. Just while I'm on this old man.
I went to a sale one time up by E-town.(5)
And they had an old car there.
Was a public sale you know.
That was back during the depression.
And they had this old car up for sale...up for
AUCTION.
And they was a-tryin' to get some bids on it.
It was an old Chevrolet.
And I seen Bill a-biddin' on the other side over there.
Well I run the car up on him.
I think I run it to seventeen dollars. Seventeen fifty
   maybe.
And Bill thought to get it bought at ten. And I run it up
   on him to SEVENTEEN-FIFTY.
And they finally knocked it off...to ME.
And...I didn't have any IDEA...didn't WANT it.
And Bill come around and give me a DOLLAR profit
on it!
And so I sold it to him.

Well it wasn't but two or three days after that
I went in the garage over here and Bill Little brought
   that car in there to Dally.(6)
And uh...the water pump was a-makin' a little noise.
And Bill says, "Dally," he says...
"Dally, I want you to work on that CAR there."
"Now," he says, "the TROUBLE
   ...the trouble is right THERE."

And he stuck his finger in that fan while the motor was
    runnin'.
He said, "the trouble's right in THERE." (Spiv laughs)
That cut a FINGER off.

I seen Dally three or four days after that and
Bill had told him...he says,
"Now I want to spend ten dollars on it, Dally."
"But," he says, "The trouble's right in there..."
(Spiv laughs again, remembering)
But you could get a water pump then for about a dollar
    and a half.
And he had a long ways to go for ten dollars.
You see what it needed was jackin' the horn up and
    runnin' a new automobile in...
That's what it needed.
Dally says...,"I worked on it the whole day.
Bill come in the next morning,"
He says, "Dally, I've changed my mind.
I wanta spend TWELVE dollars on it...instead of
TEN."
So he had some more work to do...then... you see.
And I was in there the next morning.
"Well," Dally said, "I got her done. I got her done."
He said, "My biggest job now is makin' that come out
    ten or twelve dollars!"
Yeah. "Makin' my bill come out ten or twelve
    dollars...that's my biggest job."
Well boy back then. You could just about GET a new
    automobile for twelve dollars.

And still more of Old Bill Little.

Old Bill Little...

There was a poplar TREE...now...where he lived down
along here...

And Uncle Ernest's place was practically across the
road   from him...his FARM.

And up this FENCE ROW...aww...about a couple of city
blocks...was a poplar tree.

Right in the fence row.

Now Bill Little didn't own ANYTHING on that side of
the road.

But this was a bee tree.

The bees went in just about this high.

Went in a hole.

I seen 'em...where they'd get in there.

I was a-huntin' up there and I'd seen 'em.

Well Old Wiggle.

He knew they was there TOO.

He didn't do anything but catch Bill away from
HOME...

Where he couldn't see him from down there.

Bill Little knew they was in there TOO.

And Wiggle goes up there and cuts a big notch in there
and gets all the honey out.

And where they cut this notch in this tree was right on
the side of the tree that Bill Little could set down
there on his porch and see somethin' WHITE up
there and wonder what it was.

And so he walks up there and there...they had...They'd
CUT his bee tree.

He claimed it because he'd FOUND it...you see...

Well he goes down and tells Wiggle.

And Wiggle, he was the one that CUT it.

But he was tellin' Wiggle all about somebody cuttin'
that   bee tree, and they just naturally STOLE it.

Now we was a-livin' over here at Miz Green's...I and
    Esther was.
We hadn't been married about a YEAR.
We was livin' over there.
And that little bank there along the road...we kept it
    mowed.
That crazy Wiggle.
One night...he brings some of the empty honeycomb up
    there...in squares...and dribbles it along the bank
    there.
And he sees Bill Little in a few days, he says
"I'll tell you who cut that TREE from you...and he's lost
    some of that honey off the BUCKET as he was a-
    goin' in the house."
He says, " You just look up there at that Helt's...now
    he's that guy that got that honey."
So that Bill he got all over me like a mess of measles
next   time he seen me.
I didn't know nothing about it.
Margaret: You didn't know about it?
Spiv: Heck no. (Spiv laughs) But Wiggle finally told me.
He wanted to know if I had company.
Coming up there to jump all OVER me...
Now that's what I call dirty POOL.

We used to have a lotta fun out of Bill Little.

With a little help from Pert, Spiv soon gets onto another
Scipio character.

Old John Kane over here...he lived down below the
   garage.
And he could outwalk the DEVIL when he was
NINETY years old.
And he come past the garage there one day and I was in
   there and he stopped for just a minute.
And I said, "John, I just got done tellin' Dally here, a
   few minutes ago,
If I could walk HALF as good as you're walkin' when I
   get to ninety years old,
I'll be tickled to death."
"Ahh," he said..., "that was EASY fer him."
And he went on.
And it wasn't FIVE minutes till he come back a-past
   there...
Dally was a-layin' in underneath one of them cars with
   the big door open there and he...(Spiv laughs)...
He wanted Dally to be sure and see him.
Boy he was just steppin' 'em off!
He said, "HI Dally!" (Spiv uses his best "old codger"
   voice here, then breaks off laughing.)
Old Dally's tellin' me about it and he'd just about bust
   out...
He wanted Dally to see him walkin'.

Pert, laughing: He wanted Dally to see him WALKIN'.

But Spiv has more on Old John Kane.

Spiv: We used to take him to Columbus. Years ago.
When Crescent had that old Peerless automobile.
It'd hold about...it was about a seven passenger deal.

Had two seats in the floor where you pull up and
    you...put two in there. Big dudes.
It was an old Peerless.
And he'd run like the devil.
Course that road wasn't blacktopped there...wasn't
    PAVED and it was all gravel.
Go up in the spring of the year and the WHEAT was
SO   big.
Just comin'.
Look over there and he'd say "John...?" Ain't that the
    POOREST piece of wheat that you ever seen?"
"Mnnnnnn" (mimicking old John Kane's thin
monotone whine) "never saw anything like it."
"Mnnnnn," he said, "That's the worst piece of wheat
I ever saw."
They'd go to Columbus.
They'd come back.
Cress'd look over and say, "John...? Look at that good
    piece of wheat.
Ain't that about as good a piece of wheat as you ever
    seen?"
"Mnnnnn" "I NEVER seen any BETTER."
Everyone is laughing.
Sally: Same field.
Spiv: Same field.
Esther: He just wanted to be...tied in...with whoever...
Pert: Was he the one had rheumatism in his arm...he
    couldn't get it up over his head?
Spiv (acting it out) "Mnnnnn" He said, "Mnnnnn."
Says, "just can't get 'er up like that at all."
Had it up there THEN.

Pretty soon Spiv gets onto another old codger he's remembered.

Used to be an old man here, down in the country, by the name of Barney MacFadden...used to have quite a little fun with.

He wore a black OVERCOAT...till AUGUST.

A long black overcoat.

He was a TYPICAL...Irishman.

And he never could get warm.

He was the one that was tryin' to set out tomatoes that time.

And you know a tomato's gotta have warm weather 'fore   you get him started.

He don't want...real SCALDIN' weather.

But he wants WARM weather.

You can't start one when it's cold.

And he set these tomatoes out a time or two, but he wanted to get 'em out EARLY so he could get some on the early MARKET. You see.

And...he set 'em...and reset 'em...

And he had this old big overcoat on...

And resettin' and it was cold and...

The wind blowed his hat off and took out across the tomato patch where he was settin'

And he run and got it and he says

"Snow!" "Blow!"

"STARVE a poor man to DEATH!"

(Everyone begins to laugh.)

Esther: Oooh. We've heard THAT one haven't we?

(All are laughing.)

Spiv: And that was the end of the tomato settin'.

The picture of Barney McFadden in his long black overcoat cursing the elements is one of Spiv's favorite images. His "Snow! Blow! Starve a poor man to death" has become a favorite phrase around the household...one that comes to mind whenever the weather turns against you.(7)

Spiv has more on Barney McFadden.

Spiv: Lynn Miller was a-tellin' me one time about old
    Barney...
He was a neighbor of Lynn Miller.
Big old Lynn, he used to be a wrestler, you know, and
he was big and STOUT as a BULL.
And Barney he was sick...and had been for quite a spell.
Pretty BAD.
Lynn thought...now the old fellow...might want a little
    drink of wine.
Maybe he'd...like some wine.
Well he went down.
Just a house or two.
Wasn't very far from his house.
He went down there one evening...and he said...they'd
    told him that Barney was awful bad.
Awful bad.
But he said, "I went in...and I had a quart of grape
    WINE in my overcoat pocket," he said.
And...I leaned down over...
Didn't want everybody to hear...
And I said to him
"Barney (whisper)...would you like to have a little
    swag?"
"WHAT DID YOU SAY?"
He just sat up in bed...just as QUICK.
"WHAT DID YOU SAY?"

That old big Lynn'd tell that and just die a-laughin'.
He wasn't near as dead as they THOUGHT he was.

Spiv has lots of old codger stories to tell. But after a while he pauses and reflects.

There used to be several old characters around...in the
country.
I suppose I was one OF 'em.

Everyone laughs warmly.
Esther sums it up for us:

You still ARE..you still ARE.

Spiv's old codger stories seem the most memorable part of his repertoire. When I asked my father about Spiv's stories he rattled off a list of stories of old fellows who used to live around Scipio that I should ask Spiv about. Sally begins a storytelling session by asking Spiv for a story she recalls about Bill Little. When I came to tape Spiv's stories, this was the genre that was offered first.

To be an old character one need only have some marked characteristics which lend themselves to the storyteller's art.(8) Foibles and peculiarities mark one, but being an old character is not necessarily negative. Spiv and Esther seem proud to assign Spiv a place among the "old characters around here."

Studies of the local character anecdote often focus on tales of the deviant who is looked down on by society and poked fun at.(9) "They had a lot of fun out of Old Bill Little" says Spiv. But local character anecdotes can also be told about respected community members.(10) Stories told about garage owner Crescent Miller poke fun at his preoccupation with fishing. Stories about store owner Frank McConnell center on his tight-fisted, hard-working approach to life. And stories about surveyor Charlie Butler mock his high-falutin' college educated ways.

It seems, however, that tales of the in-group deviant who is weird enough to be labeled an oddity are those first told and most repeated. These tales best serve the purposes of the group as it evaluates itself, sets the bounds of normal society, and points out the weirdest of them all. There is always a slight twinge of "there-but-for-the-grace-of-God-go-I" in these stories.(11)

The community seems proud in a way of its old codgers. There is even a kind of immorality in being an "oddity".(12) When I asked folks what Scipio was like in the old days, they usually responded by telling me about some of Scipio's "characters." These local characters form a focal point for memories of the old times, functioning somewhat as mnemonic devices for the recall of community history. History must be peopled to matter. By keeping these stories alive the memories of the old time Scipio linger on a little longer.

Spiv's tales of old codgers and oddities then function not only to provide entertainment, they often serve a scapegoat function and define the outer limits of community behavior through labeling of the in-group deviant. They also preserve bits of community history through their very memorable nature. The entire group "owns" these tales and in a special way they contribute to community identity and community solidarity.(13)

NOTES
CHAPTER 7

1. 7/6/78. Evening, Helt's back porch. Gordon and Esther, Gordon's brother, Pert Helt and wife Sally, and Margaret MacDonald.
2. Benjamin Kuhn of Hartsville relates a tale of cats attacking a corpse and adds, "Now you know that cats will attack a dead body, or so I've always heard." (p. 191). Donald Allport Bird and James R. Dow, "Benjamin Kuhn: Life and Narratives of a Hoosier Farmer," *Indiana Folklore* 5, No. 2, (1982): 143-260.
3. See Mary Douglas, "The Social Control of Cognition: Some Factors in Joke Perception," *Man*, New Series, 3 no. 3, (Sept. 1968): 361-376 for a brief but interesting discussion of the role of the joker at a funeral (pp. 373-374).
4. Ben Kuhn also uses this term. "Had a lot of fun out of Tom Benton" (Bird and Dow, p. 178). the phrase is interestingly parallel to the phrase "I had a lot of good out of ..." as in "I had a lot of good out of this hat." Both phrases denote usage of sorts. If we "had a lot of fun out of Old Bill Little," why we put him to some good use it seems.
5. Elizabethtown, Indiana.
6. Dallas Clark.
7. For discussion of the humorous catch phrase as it functions in one Jennings County Indiana family, see Margaret Read MacDonald, "It Don't Take Long to Look at a Horseshoe: The Humorous Anecdote Catch-Phrase as Proverbial Saying" (Indiana Folklore and Oral History, 15, No. 2, (1986): 95-120.
8. Sandra K. D. Stahl in her article "The Local Character Anecdote" *Genre* 8 no. 4, (December 1975): 283-302 notes that "The one important function of the local character anecdote is the characterization of the local character." An anecdote is retained in the community "because it records just the kind of thing that 'character' would do, given his particular personality." (p. 294)
9. See "Chapter 7, Local Character Anecdotes" in Patrick B. Mullen, *I Heard the Old Fisherman Say: Folklore of the Texas Gulf Coast*, (Austin & London: University of Texas, 1984), pp. 113-129.
10. Irving Goffman in *Stigma: Notes on the Management of Spoiled Identity* (Englewood Cliffs, N.J.: Prentice-Hall, 1963), p.141 notes that "It is known that a confirmed high position in some small close-knit groups can be associated with a license to deviate and hence to be a

deviator. The relation of such a deviator to the group and the conception members have of him are such as to withstand restructuring by virtue of the deviation."

11. Kai T. Erikson ("Notes on the Sociology of Deviance" in *Deviance: The Interactionist Perspective*, ed. by Earl Rumington and Martin S. Weinberg, (New York: Macmillan, 1978) discussed the importance of the deviant as a definer of boundaries for the group. "The visible deviant...as a trespasser against the group norms, he represents those forces which lie outside the group's boundaries: he informs us, as it were, what evil looks like, what shapes the devil can assume. And in doing so, shows us the difference between the inside of the group and the outside...Thus deviance cannot be dismissed simply as behavior which *disrupts* stability in society, but may itself be, in controlled quantities, an important condition for *preserving* stability..." (pp. 28-29).

For a useful discussion of the local character as deviant see Patrick B. Mullen, I Heard the Old Fisherman Say. Mullen says of the eccentric character tale, "The verbalization of the incident is a part of the process of labeling a person as a deviant. After the person is no longer around, the stories continue to be told, and they continue to function to label the behavior described in them as deviant." (p. 117)

12. Of Patrick B. Mullen's slightly retarded and definitely uncouth Taylor brothers, subject of local character anecdotes on the Texas Gulf Coast, folks said, "There's thousands of people know worlds of them and there's thousands of tales that could be told." "I guess Mac and Harvey was known by more people than any person that's ever been on the Texas coast." (p. 119) Patrick B. Mullen *I Heard the Old Fisherman Say: Folklore of the Texas Gulf Coast*, (Austin & London: University of Texas Press, 1984).

13. Levette J. Davidson, writing of the Gassy Thompson anecdotes says that "Their stories served, during the period when they were orally current, to increase the attachment of both narrator and listener to the community. Such characters and such stories contributed...and still contribute...gaiety to small town life." quoted in Sandra K.D. Stahl, "The Local Character Anecdote," <u>Genre</u> 8 no. 4, (December 1975): 295; Patrick B. Mullen (ibid.) concludes "The anecdotes about real deviants become the property of the entire group, and as such they can function more effectively than traditional tales as symbolic expressions of that particular community's values and norms." (p. 129).

Now this first one is Kutch...the next one's Clint
Hammond...the next one is Gividen...
the next one is Coons...the next one is John Carnes. Now
we've got one, two, three...what about Coons, is he dead?...
Three dead out of *that* bunch(1).
Margaret: What were they doin' there?
Spiv: Kutch is just a loafin'...
and Clint he just stopped in to buy a little something...
and the other three worked on the county highway. It was
noon...
chances are it was noon...you see.
Esther: And see these boxes in front of the store...
that was to sit on too.
Spiv: And that was the store that we put the bread boxes
around old George Waughtel. Put 'em *inside*!
But that's one of my prize pictures.

*   *   *

CHAPTER 8
PRANKING AT THE STORE AND OTHER PRACTICAL JOKES

Local character anecdotes, practical joking in Scipio, and the scene at the general stores around 1920-30. These topics usually cluster together in Spiv's talk. A lot of fun was had at the general stores through playing practical jokes on Scipio's oddities, telling stories about them, and generally poking fun at them. Poking fun and playing jokes usually ended up by giving the Scipio storytellers even more grist for their mill.

Spiv's old codger stories were probably honed into shape at the store and most of his local character tales wind back to Scipio town sooner or later as his character meets up with the fellows at the store or the garage.

Scipio's older folks tell me over and over that in the old days folks had to "make their own fun." Perhaps in those days before radio serials and TV sitcoms, they had to "make their own stories" too.

* * *

PRANKING AT THE STORE

At nine every morning Jeanette Kelly unlocks the front door of the Scipio General Store. She switches on the lights, unlocks the cash register, and is ready to handle the trade of Scipio's day. Since Milholland's store burned in 1956 this has been the only store in Scipio. Wilson's Corner, six miles to the north has a similar small all-purpose grocery and four miles south just where the now abandoned Pennsylvania railroad bed crosses Highway 7, is an even tinier grocery stop. For more extensive shopping, you have to drive to North Vernon or Columbus.

Jeanette does a slow but steady trade in small items at the store. Not enough to get rich on, but enough to keep the store open. About noon Duc Hoppus wanders up the block from his small house down on Water Street, and after a while George Henry drifts on in too.

George Henry and Duc Hoppus are doing their part to keep alive a tradition as much a part of Scipio's character as the school and church up the street. Loafing down at the store has been a basic part of Scipio life since the store first opened. Used to be the loafing was done by a much larger crew though.

Back in the 20s and 30s Kutch McConnell held Saturday night drawings and huge crowds would come into town. After Crescent Miller rigged up his own generator and brought electricity to all of downtown Scipio, Kutch installed a radio set and folks would come from all around to listen to the radio on Saturday evenings down at McConnell's store.

Scipio had two general stores back then. Just a half block up the main drag from the business-minded

McConnell store was Milholland's, run by easy-going Willard Milholland. Willard had an infectious laugh and a mandolin behind the counter. So the Scipio crowd had a choice of residences in those days.

Stories of the goings on at McConnell's and Milholland's stores form a basic part of Scipio's storytelling repertoire. The details of these episodes are community knowledge. As Spiv said of one of Helen McConnell's stories about old John Andy Day, "I've heard her tell it a *hundred* times." Esther agreed. "So have *I*...so have *I*."(2)

Spiv and Esther tell about Old George Waughtel and the evening crowd at McConnell's and Milholland's long about 1933.(3)

Spiv: Tell 'bout...What the boys used to do on Old
George Waughtel(4) when he'd come over to the
store there and pile them boxes around him.
I told you that one last year.

He was an old man...
Had whiskers down about like this
And he'd come in the store there and had a cane...
And he'd always set that cane down...
Just kind of set on it...you know.
Esther: Leaned on it...and go to sleep.
Spiv: Yeah he wouldn't be there a minute till he'd be
asleep.
And he'd sleep all the time he was over there.
And they was always a bunch in there...a-loafin'.
Be eight or ten.
And Kutch...as long as Kutch could sell a nickel's worth
of candy or a package of cigarettes...he'd stay
open.

And eleven o'clock at night...he'd...
Esther: No closing time.
Spiv: No closing time.
As long as...
Esther: As long as there was anybody there...
Spiv: So we was in there one night...
Back then you got all that old groceries in big old boxes
    and stuff.
Big old pasteboard boxes.
Bread came in boxes, you know. And everything.
Esther: And he hardly ever threw anything away.
Spiv: Never threw NOTHING away.
And we went out there and...we was gettin' ready to
    leave...
We just built a PEN around old George.
Out of these boxes.
Up high.
Esther: Went back in Frank's back room...
Spiv: And got 'em all out of there.
Built a pen around him.
Just out a little piece.

And boy when he got up...
The old man could cuss a blue streak anyhow.
When he got up...
And run into them...
They all fell in on him!

He nearly cussed everybody in Scipio.

He quit goin' down there.
He wouldn't go down there anymore.
But he just...came up to Willard's(5).

Well Willard didn't stay open as late.---
But he always had...Willard had a great big old stove
  back
Here at the back
And had quite a little space in behind it.
And old George would always get in the corner.
Esther: Had chairs around so they could loaf.
Spiv: Yeah...everybody...would LOAF around there,
  you know.
And this old door...of Willard's store...had about that
  much PLAY.
You could just...(Spiv demonstrates shaking the door
  and feeling it move)
Esther: Both doors was like that.
Spiv: Well they'd been locked and unlocked a jillion
  times, you know.
Esther: And Willard...ever time he'd...
Spiv: He'd be sure it was locked.
He'd jerk on that like that...
Esther: That's what caused the door to...
Spiv: You'd think he wasn't goin' to QUIT.
He'd just keep...(He SHAKES more doors) to be sure it
  was locked.

Well now Willard...
The old feller come up there to Willard's one night.
And he'd been in there a million times, you know.
Ever night he's come over.
And Willard...
Settin' back there asleep.
Willard locked that store.
Esther: And forgot him.
Spiv: And forgot him.

He just...didn't do it a-purpose.

Esther: Willard wouldn't do it on purpose I don't think.

Spiv: Noo.

And he said "I got over home and sit down there in the chair and was readin' the paper a little while...

And I could hear that...heard that door..."

(Spiv breaks out laughing)

Esther: Lived right across the street.

Spiv: "My God," he says.

Come to him right away.

"I know what's the matter.

I've locked GEORGE in!"

And he went over there and I guess when that old man got done with Willard...

Esther: The air was BLUE.

Spiv: Cause he'd just got locked up BELOW there six months before.

Esther: He'd been PENNED up down there.

Spiv: And LOCKED up up here.

And Willard told me.

He said, "I...I wouldn't of done it to that old man for anything."

But he said, "I...just FORGOT about him."

And he said, "I never did make that old man believe that I didn't lock him in there on purpose."

(Spiv chuckles to himself as the story trails off.)

The country store was a main point of assimilation for the "oddity" in the community.(6) Here his oddities were the object of joking by other men. Here he was "appreciated" for the fun they had over him, if for nothing else. Spiv tells of old Bob Van Dusen and his prospecting.

Spiv: Over here at the store one night...(7)
He was always a huntin'...huntin' gold.
He was a prospector.
He came over here at McConnell's store one night.
You've seen this gold that's in coal...haven't you?
Margaret: Yeah...that "fool's gold?"(8)
Spiv: Yeah. He found some of that someplace.
And he come in the store over there one night...one
    evening...
Just about this time of evening.
And they never closed till midnight, you know.
And there was a whole BUNCH in there.
Toot Greathouse and I don't know...
Hube Walsh...
And I don't know who ALL was in there.
And they got to talkin' about...asked him how he'd
done.
And if he'd found anything that day.
And he said, "Yes I DID."
And there was a salesman in the bunch, see.
I don't know what he was a-sellin' but there was a
    salesman in that bunch around there.
And everybody...he was a-showin' it to 'em...
And just kinda goin' around...
"Boy...I'd jist kinda like to know where you found that
    at."
He said, "I ain't tellin' ya.
That's one thing that the old Bob's a-gonna keep to
    HIMSELF."
And he'd go to the next one.
"Boys," he said, "that there..." That looks good to HIM.
"Where'd you FIND that at, Bob?"
"I ain't a-tellin' ye."

And uh...come in this salesman.
He didn't KNOW him, you see?
He looked it all over and he said,
"Well...I'll tell ya.
That looks like damn fool's gold to ME."
"By God," Bob said,
"There's a lotta damn fools like to know where I
    FOUND it, anyhow!"

Bob's reaction to the salesman's accusation that his gold is fake suggests that Bob may have known he had fool's gold all the time and that he knew that everyone knew it was fool's gold. It was the "game" and the attention he was enjoying. A game which the salesman--the outsider--had broken. When confronted, Bob cleverly turns the tables and names his tormentors as the *real* fools.

There was a time when telling stories down at the store was a high art form in Scipio.(9) Playing pranks seems to have been an art form too. And then as we've said, a good prank certainly makes a good *story.*(10)

ON PRACTICAL JOKING

Stories of practical jokes seem to form a large part of Spiv's storytelling repertoire.(11) As we have seen, many of Spiv's old codger tales involve practical joking or, at least, putting the other fellow on. Spiv is seldom the joke player in these stories.(12) I guess Spiv wouldn't normally do something like that to a fellow himself but he sure enjoys retelling these stories.

Pranking is often a community test of temperament. Spiv delights in this story of the preacher's son stealing watermelons. When the Wileys' boy worked at the creamery up at Columbus, a preacher's boy was working with them.

Spiv: And they'd get to telling 'bout things that had happened to Them when they was BOYS...(13)
And there was a preacher's boy worked there too.
And he said, "Boy, that's somethin' I never did do."
Said, "The next time you fellers go to steal
    watermelons."
He said, "Let me know."
"I wanta go WITH you."

So...Herman Long...he knew Bill Faudry.
And Bill always had about eight or ten acres of
    watermelons down there just off 31...there in the
    sand.(14)
And he goes to Bill...that night...and tells him...
Says, "Now Bill. We're gonna come in...down there in
    your watermelon patch tomorrow night...after dark.
And we're gonna steal some watermelons.
And we want you...
To be down there with the shotgun.
And when I get ready to light...when I light my
    cigarette..."
He said, "We GOT a big one and we're gettin' ready to
    leave.
And we'll be talkin' kinda low...and you can tell where
    we're AT.
We want you to get right behind us..."

Well. That's what happened.
Mutt lit the cigarette and old Bill...fellow that owned the
    flats...

He shot that old shotgun in the air...
And he said, "Talk about runnin'..."
He said, "You never saw a bunch run any harder in
your   life."
And Mutt...
Mutt had a sack o'...pocket full of soy beans.
And ever time he'd shoot...Old Mutt'd give that
     preacher's boy a load of soy beans!
That's the way the story ended up.
Them a-throwin' soy beans at him when they'd shoot
     that shotgun.
Esther closes the story off: They're still a-runnin', I
     guess.
When I asked Spiv why they'd do something like that to
a feller, he just laughed. "Well he wanted to GO.
And...he was a PREACHER'S son."

Spiv launched into a story of Snipe Hunting. "You've heard them talk about Snipe Huntin'. Held the bag. They used to do that quite a bit...and they...get some greenhorn...who didn't know what he was a-doin'...take him out there and just leave him *stand* in the dark. Then slip off someplace and they'd be smokin' a cigarette...laughin'."

The victim had to be a greenhorn...either pretty naive or not too bright. "Now you take somebody that's pretty up on his toes...they can't devil him as much because he catches *on* quick."

The preacher's son's watermelon stealing can be considered something in the way of an initiation. The preacher's son himself probably laughed about it afterwards. But some of the pranking in Scipio is just plain *mean*, there is no getting around it.(15)

There seems to be a strong tendency to devil the fellow who's *not* up on his toes. When I asked Spiv whether one of their joke butt's did not get angry, he said no. "He didn't catch *on*." Continued joking at the expense of the not-too-bright oddball who doesn't quite catch on certainly has its negative aspects. There is always a tendency to scapegoat the fellow who carries to extremes in his person all of the negative traits which we sense in ourselves in lesser quantities. A well-established scapegoat in the group takes a load off everyone's shoulders. As long as the group already has a fool and a dummy *we* are safe.

In a way the telling of funny stories on a fellow can be positive rather than negative.(16) It brings his faults out in the open, allows the community to consider his shortcomings openly and laugh them off. While the discomfort of the moment may be considerable, the overall effect of this joking may be that of allowing him to remain an accepted part of the community. The stress of having to cope with a misfit within the community is defused through laughter. The community in a sense "owns" him as one of their own problems through their elevation of him to a joking-butt status. The joke victim who is able to see the humor of the situation and laugh at himself, may find that his role as butt of the joke allows him to maintain a tolerated place within the group.

If the butt of the joke is *not* able to see the humor in his own plight, or worse yet if the joke ruse is never discovered by the butt...the outcome may be more negative. The defusing function of the joke playing is still in effect, but the joke butt does not play his part in return by acknowledging his role. By failing to "play" he consigns *himself* to the role of outsider.

The main difference between the boxing of old John Waughtel and the planting of honey on Spiv's lawn is the reaction of the prank's butt. Scipio's pranking is not confined to the oddball or the greenhorn, it is a much practiced art for use on one's buddies as well. The difference being that one's buddies generally are "good sports" and "can take a joke."(17)

Your response to the group's teasing defines you; it tells us what you are like, and places you in relationship to your group. It also defines *us*...tells us just how different Scipio folks can get, and outlines the limits of behavior in this community. Scipio hangs onto the memory of its "characters" with something like pride. These tales show that strange things are possible.

Pranking, joking and the stories which result are one of the community's ways to define itself. It is through stories that the community formulates its feelings, stores them, and talks to itself about the way it feels.

NOTES:
CHAPTER 8

1. Gordon Helt, Esther Helt, Margaret MacDonald looking at slides at Gordon and Esther's house, January 18th, 1983 in the evening. Men in photo are (right to left): Frank McConnell, Clint Hammond, Maurice Gividen, George Coons, Jack Carnes.
2. Gordon and Esther Helt, 1/16/83.
3. Gordon and Esther Helt at their house, telling to Margaret MacDonald, 1/16/83.
4. Pronounced "Walk-tl."
5. Willard Milholland, owner of the *other* store.
6. Goffman speaks of the "in-group deviant": "A member who deviates whether in deed or in the attributes he possesses, or both, and in consequence comes to play a special role, becoming a symbol of the group and a performer of certain clownish functions, even while he is denied the respect accorded full-fledged members...He is often the focus of attention that welds others into a participating circle around him, even while it strips him of some of the status of a participant." (pp. 141-142). Erving Goffman, *Stigma: Notes on the Management of Spoiled Identity,* (Englewood Cliffs, NJ: Prentice-Hall, 1963).
7. Gordon Helt to Margaret MacDonald and wife Esther Helt, 1/4/84.
8. Pyrite. Common in slate in this area.
9. Richard Bauman discusses talk at the La Have Island General Store in Nova Scotia as a setting marked with the aesthetic function. "The session at the store is singled out as special, isolated from the others and enjoyed for its own sake, because talking there may be enjoyed for its own sake and not as part of another activity or for some instrumental purpose. In other words, the fact that this situation is set aside for sociability, pure and simple, makes it special. We might say that the islanders have singled out this speech situation and marked it with what Murkarovsky calls the esthetic function, which isolates or foregrounds the activity itself, causes a maximum focusing of attention upon it and endows it with the ability to evoke pleasure in the participants." The heyday of La Have Island General Store talk was apparently over by the late 1930s and Bauman is working from the remembrances of old-timers. His theory that the setting itself had been endowed by the community with an esthetic function seems applicable to the Scipio general store tellings as well. All of these stories which

occurred at the store are undoubtedly drawn from the general store tellers' repertoire of that time. (pp. 340-341) Richard Bauman, "The La Have Island General Store: Sociability and Verbal Art in a Nova Scotia Community," *Journal of American Folklore* 85 No. 338 (Oct-Dec. 1972): 330-343; Bauman is citing Jan Mukarovsky, *Aesthetic Function, Norm and Value as Social Facts*, trans. Mark E. Suino. (Ann Arbor MI, 1970), pp. 21-22.

10. In Kay Cothran's discussion of practical joking, she notes that "No doubt such jokes are really played, but much of the fun is in the later narration..." p. 348. Kay Cothran, "Talking Trash in the Okefenokee Swamp Rim, Georgia," *Journal of American Folklore*, 87, no. 346, (Oct-Dec. 1974): 340-356.

11. Richard S. Tallman notes that "Practical joke stories that are traditional to a folk group represent only the tip of the iceberg, the iceberg being the tradition of playing practical jokes." For interesting discussion of practical joking and pranking, see *Southern Folklore Quarterly*, 38, no. 4, (December 1974). The entire issue is devoted to this topic and Tallman's article "A Generic Approach to the Practical Joke," pp. 253-259 is especially useful.

12. Richard S. Tallman points out that the narrator invariably sees himself as a part of the practical joke tradition. He suggests that "Most often...the narrator is or was a part of the group but was not an actor in the event being described...The further removed the narrator is from the actual event, the more broadly traditional and less esoteric the story becomes, but likewise, the practical joke event then becomes less specific, less traditional as something that actually happened." (p. 273) Richard S. Tallman, "A Generic Approach to the Practical Joke," *Southern Folklore Quarterly*, 38, no. 4, (December 1974): 259-274.

13. 10/10/82. Sunday afternoon drive with Spiv and Esther down by Vernon. (Story collected also 1/17/83 while driving past scene of story between Scipio and Reddington with Spiv.)

14. Highway 31.

15. Kay Cothran, in her article "Talking Trash in the Okefenokee Swamp Rim" notes that "Through old Southwestern humor, both literary and oral, runs a strong strain of humor involving cruelty and discomfiture." (p. 348)

16. John R. Scott's discussion of joking among the Newfoundland seal fishermen suggests that a basic function of pranks and practical jokes is that of "general entertainment." He sees them also, however, as a means of releasing hostility and controlling behavior. John R. Scott,

"Practical Jokes of the Newfoundland Seal Fishery," *Southern Folklore Quarterly*, 38, no. 4, (December 1974): 275-283.

17. John R. Bowman's study of practical jokes played by college students concludes that "such jokes are usually limited to close friends and family members"...people who "are likely to take the prank playfully." (p. 71) John R. Bowman, "On Getting Even: Notes on the Organization of Practical Jokes," in *The Paradoxes of Play*, Proceedings of the 69th annual meeting of the Association for the Anthropological Study of Play, edited by John W. Loy, (West Point NY, Leisure Press, 1982), pp. 65-75. Joking patterns in a community may show repeated pranks pulled on certain good natured souls of high status and visibility. See Roger Welsch's discussion of practical joking among folklorists, for example. Roger L. Welsch, "A Note on Practical Jokes," *Southern Folklore Quarterly*, 38, no. 4, (December 1974): 253-258. Richard Tallman's "Classificatory Checklist for the Study of the Practical Joke" (Richard S. Tallman, "A Generic Approach to the Practical Joke, " *Southern Folklore Quarterly*, 38, no. 4, (December 1974): 259-274 seems to lack this concept of the 'victim' as 'esteemed-able-to-take-it-colleague.' Tallman's classification of victims includes "individual traditionally joked (traditional dupe or fool; outsider)," "initiate" and "individual not traditionally joked" but seems to lack a classification for in-group members who are traditionally joked.

CHAPTER 9
CITY SLICKERS

Another laughable character for the storyteller's art is the city slicker.(1) The city slicker who moves into the country has always been viewed with suspicion. And often rightly so. City folks seldom stick around long. They may move out into the country on a lark when some big firm brings them into a nearby town to manage a factory or handle some important job. But after a couple of years they move on.

And the brainy guy who descends on the community with a get-rich-scheme to sell his new neighbors is not unknown in Scipio. One fellow came in and made a big stir in the 1950's. He built a housing subdivision just north of Scipio, and opened up an instant-house production plant on Highway 7, about five miles north of town, building houses in two halves and trucking them to the buyer's lot. He came up with a big investment scheme and talked a lot of folks around here into chipping in a few thousand dollars. The stock at last word was worth about seven cents on the dollar. The Entrepeneuer, on the other hand, seems to have come out okay, with Motels spread all over the country.

Scipio residents speak ruefully of their gullibility in buying into this scheme. No particular bitterness. They should have known better. They just laugh weakly and chalk it up to experience.

Spiv seldom has much contact with citified folks. But occasionally somebody with more education than brains moves into the Scipio area and begins to neighbor. Most of Spiv's city slicker stories deal with Scipio-born fellows who go off to school or big city jobs and come back "educated."

Spiv: They was telling about the Butler's over here...(2)
Well I must have been around thirty...thirty-five...
Charlie came over here one morning--that was YOUNG
     Charlie--
See there was an old Charlie Butler that run the depot
     over here.
And his son...lived over here and he was an army
officer.
And he...had a pretty good education.
He was a surveyor too.
And he drove...now you can't remember this because it
     was before your time.
He drove an old Dodge...sedan--and they always had
     what we called...a bastard gear shift.
Because it was just opposite from the standard gear
     shift.
Your low was here...and your reverse was up above...
And...just BACKWARDS.
Well he wasn't very much of a mechanic.
Never had much experience only in the army.
And that was office work mostly.
Esther: College too, he was pretty educated...in college.
Spiv: That's what I say...

Yeah he had a pretty good education, but he wasn't too
  smart when it came to everyday life.
And he'd drive that old Dodge...and he'd be goin'
  along...goin' along...just a-talkin' and all at once
  start shiftin' gears.
Shift gear...you know.
And then go again.
And it was all...
All UNCALLED for.
But that was the kind of fella he was.
He called me one time and they had some chickens over
  here
And he...he's come over and he said,
"Spiv...there's somethin' got in the chickens last night."
And he says, "they've killed about all of them."
And he wanted me to come over and see what...
He says, "It's an OWL."
"I know," he says, "It's an OWL."
Well I picked up...about a dozen steel traps and I went
  over there...I FIGURED it was a mink.
He says, "They didn't carry them off, they just killed
  'em."
Mink always catches 'em by the throat here and sucks
  the blood all out...they just fall over dead.
And I went over there and sure enough.

Spiv traps the mink, but this reminds him of another
  story.
But there was another one happened right there.
That uh...TOM Butler. That was HIS boy.
He got married...and was ALL education and no
  experience.
And uh...she was too. His wife.

Hadn't been married but a short time.
And it was in August.
HOT. It was HOT.
And uh...they come over here one evening
And uh...all excited and...wanted me to come over there.
That they had killed something...and they thought it
was   a skunk.
And uh...it was one of them old straggly looking things.
(Spiv chuckles at the thought of the beast)
And it wasn't a very big one at that.
And she wanted me...
If I could clean...er SKIN it.
And make her a set of FURS out of it.
(We all laugh)
A set of FURS.
Margaret (missing the point): That'd smell good,
wouldn't it?
Spiv: Well...they MAKE 'em.
They make 'em out of them.
But anyhow...
In AUGUST...
There wasn't a dozen hairs on it! (Spiv laughs)
They don't hair out and get fur on it till the frost
    starts a-fallin'. ---
Esther: They didn't get you to skin it, did they?
Spiv: No. I would've...if it'd been...in season...you know.
If it'd have any fur on it---but JIMINY.

You take an old POSSUM.
Anything.
Specially an old possum...in the summertime.
Why he ain't got enough hair on him to...
The hair all falls off.

Because...that keeps him COOL.
If he had the same set of fur on there he had in January
  why he'd smother to death in the summertime.
Nature takes care of that, you see.
And uh...they didn't know it...
They didn't know it...
They'd never lived...(Spiv breaks off in laughter at the
  ignorance of "educated" folks)

The "educated" feller usually displays his ignorance
through showing off his newly acquired vocabulary.
Sometimes it backfires.

Spiv: Well Pig (Kane) over here worked for Bob
  Amick.(3)
And he lived over there just the other side of Margaret's
  (Ryan).
Go over the hump and go in there.
Well there's this barn lot. There's about half acre in it.
Big barn...big old barn.
Now this wasn't yesterday.
Because Pig was young and had plenty of go in him.
And Chester come down there...from college...or some
  big...job, you know.
Using great big words...
And of course Pig never went to school...(Spiv laughs)
Esther: He didn't understand all them words, did he?
(She is laughing) Only the kind HE used. (Apparently
  rough language!)
Spiv: They had this bad bull.
And they was gonna take him to the city. See.
And they got him out of the pasture.
And got him in the barn lot.

He wouldn't go in the barn.
And they had a fence come up here like that.
He got in that corner.
And they was all out here, you see.
He just got in beside the barn...and held up his old head
    there and looked...
And looked right back at 'em...you see.
And Chester, I reckon, was directing the thing...I don't
    know.
But, he said, "Pig APPROACH him."
(Spiv laughs) Pig didn't know what "approach" was.
He [Chester] said, "Approach him!"
"By God!" Pig said, "If you want him 'approached'
'Approach' him yourself!"
(We are all laughing over this.)
Margaret Ryan adds: Oh, he was a MEAN one.
He had Pig's Dad up there in one of them trees...
One of them trees over there and he had to STAY there.

The city feller who is a good sport can still be an
accepted member of the community despite his city
connection. Spiv tells a funny story on his brother-in-law,
Edgar Green. Though Edgar grew up in Scipio, he moved
to Indianapolis after he finished high school and is
considered a "city" resident.

Spiv: I was gonna tell you about old Edgar Green.(4)
They come down...(from Indianapolis)...over Saturday
    night and we went out to Fitzpatrick's.
We's a-goin' a-COON huntin'.
I had a pretty good coon dog.
And boy it was thawed out. It was muddy.
Boy those fields were awful muddy.---

He [Edgar] didn't want to go so bad...but Fitz wanted
 him to go.
And uh..."Awww"...he didn't have no overshoes...
And "Awww" Fitz says "I'll get you a pair of overshoes.
 There'll be one around the house there that them
 boys was a-wearin,'"
 he says, "That'll fit you."
And they was...
They was outdoor overshoes.
They wasn't indoor overshoes.
They was out...bout...bout THAT wide
And come to 'bout THERE, you know...
And he put 'em on...and they was just about a size and a
 half too big fer him.
Just "flop" "flop" on him.
And we went...down across the field and the old dog
 treed.
Went down there and he'd got him a coon.
We got him.
And he was a dog like that...he (Fitz) didn't know where
 he was at.
Man when he...he was always a-huntin'...but you didn't
 know WHERE he was at.
And he was just as liable to tree a half mile south...or a
 half a mile north of ya...
You wouldn't know.
Till he treed.
Well then he'd tree possums too.
And there was quite a few possums back then.
And that old feller...he'd tree again waaay down
through there...
And...course we knew the territory, I and Fitz did,
 but Ed...he didn't know WHERE he was a-goin'.

He didn't know whether he was goin' to run into a
    sinkhole...or a rattlesnake...er what not...
    and the ground was soft.
And...we went ALL OVER that country
And I don't know how many old possums we caught
And we caught two coons that night.

Well it was...we got about a mile and a half from home.
And the road was soft (muddy) too.
Come out to the road.
And we decided...it was about twelve o'clock at night
you   see...by that time...We left just after dark.
We decided we'd come HOME.
And the car...was a mile and a half from us.
We started down...the road...
And we was a-talkin'...and he was a-draggin' them big
    old overshoes...
And he wasn't used to that...
And uh...we git just...about home...
And we heard that old dog...gnawing!
Treed again!

Well we took down over the field there...
And he didn't know whether to...what to do...
But he wasn't no QUITTER...
And he stayed WITH us.
And went up there...he had an old possum there.

We got back...to the road...and we finally got in.
It was 'round one o'clock when we got in.

And he never did forget that.
I heard him tell that ever once in a while.

He'd say, "Boy...that was the worst I ever felt in my
 life."
Margaret: He wasn't in the habit of huntin'?
Spiv: NO...he wasn't.
He lived at Indianapolis you know.
He didn't work...I mean HUNT.
But that liked to killed him.
If he was here he could really tell you ever...CORNER
of it.
I didn't remember it so well...I was gettin' a kick out of
 it...
Not HIM.

Just as he is suspicious of the city dweller, Spiv realizes
the city folks may have less than charitable opinions of
rural folks. Spiv doesn't lose much sleep over this. He'd
have a quick answer if anyone tried to put *him* down as a
rube.

Spiv: They told Susie [a niece]...when she went
 over...moved over in Pennsylvania...---that she
 TALKED funny.(5)
The fellow in the lab [where she worked] did.
They wanted to know if they had TELEVISION back in
 Indiana yet.
(We all laugh at such teasing)
If that'd been me I'd a said first thing
"Yessir! We got that RIGHT after Dad got the
Cadillac."
"Yeah my Dad drives an old Cadillac. Gets a new one
 every year."
I'd a made him feel funny some way.
And I wouldn't a-been a-kiddin' ye EITHER.

Esther: That's right. He's got a Cadillac.
Spiv: Gets one every YEAR.

My father, Murray Read, is a close friend of Spiv's. I asked him about the Scipio's attitude toward city folks.

Murray: Well...I...I suppose that the negative
   characteristics that people would have...
   would be their attitude...of tryin' to make other
   people feel inferior to THEM.(6)
Feel that they was BETTER than somebody...some
   other people...
And...so many times the people from the city do feel...
That they are...superior.
That the country folks are ignorant.
That they don't KNOW much.
That...they FEEL that.
And then...of course...they come to the...country area...
   and try to make you FEEL that way.
I know...we used to go to the family reunions...
You notice it so much...around a gathering where city
   people and country people are gathered together.
The city people come down...and...
Now like the men...a whole bunch of the men will be
   standin' around talkin'.
Well those fellows from the city...will be runnin' off
   their head about the big automobiles...and how fast
   they drive and all that kind of stuff, you know.
Just a big impression like they was the big shots.
And talking about their big business deals...and all that
   stuff, you know...Just a-blurtin' out...Their old
   chest stickin' out...and just a-runnin' off at the
   head.

And you could just line up and TELL 'em, you know.

You know they just run off at the head and make you
think that they was ...the biggest shots at
Indianapolis...or wherever they lived...and they'll
come down there...
And their wives...will stop at the grocery store on their
way down...and buy a pound or two of bananas or
half a dozen oranges or something like that and
bring...to the pitch-in dinner.

And eat all the fried chicken and good food they can eat
and pies and cakes and then take a plate and fill it
up. With all this fried chicken and cake and
stuff...two or three plates and take it home with
them to eat.

Now they're the kind of people that's CITY.
CITY PEOPLE...you see.
That's the way they DO.
And that's...you know...you can just...pick 'em OUT.
And make you feel like...that you was a little old
ignorant   nincompoop...or nothin'.
But I noticed it at the family reunions and the
gatherins...WHEREVER the city people and the
country people are gathered together...you just
notice the same thing.
Now a lot of people might not notice that.
But, Boy, I tell ya I do.

I asked Murray about certain folks who had moved to
Jennings County and became good citizens.

Murray: Oooh land!
There's a lot of nice people...come to the little towns
    from the city.
There are a lot of nice people.
Awful nice people.
Yeah...there's nothin' wrong with them.
At all.
They're not all...no they're not all bad...
    just because they come from the city...not at all.
Lot of nice people.
Just because you come from the city don't necessarily
    make you BAD.
But you do...have a tendency to look 'em over pretty
    close.
If they come there...and drivin' a big automobile...
Makin' a big splurge...and givin' the impression that
    they're better than you are and all that kind of
    stuff...
You gotta look 'em over pretty CAREFULLY before
    you have any dealings with them.

Scipio does not want outsiders in its midst. It is glad
enough to see new folks move into the community, but it
wants to assimilate them as soon as possible. They are
invited to church, folks try to get to know them, to find out
as much as possible about them. If they respond favorably,
they soon become members of the community and are no
longer "outsider." Scipio prefers to deal with the threat of
the alien in its midst by inclusion rather than exclusion. A
favorite religious poem reads "He drew a circle that shut
me out. Heretic, rebel, a thing to flout. But love and I had
the wit to win. We drew a circle that took him in."(7) Only

if this attack fails, is the newcomer permanently labeled as an "outsider" and marked off of the map of community members.(8)

NOTES:
CHAPTER 9

1. Gene Bluestein in *The Voice of the Folk: Folklore and American Literary Theory* discusses the country-city tension and the historical tensions between "rough" Americans and European "high" culture. Bluestein credits Constance Rourke with "awareness of the major strategy which Americans have utilized to establish their own sense of identity and coherence...She noted the significant function of comedy as a way of blunting the criticism of European high cultures." "Moreover it makes us aware of the persistent use of the mark of persona as the characteristic response to foreign criticism. The barbarism of the Americans reveals itself to be a more complex state than many critics have perceived, partly because it is itself a literary strategy." (p. 80).

Bluestein uses "The Arkansas Traveler" as example and shows that "The Traveler-Squatter antagonism, which seems to be regional, masks a deeper tension between the European traveler, who is smug and condescending, and the American native, who cleverly reverses the roles. He is that barbarian whose vitality and poetic expression Emerson and Whitman so admired, and his essential defense against gentility is a trenchant humor." (p. 85)

Bluestein's comments help set Scipio's deep-seated anti-city-slicker mode in historical perspective, point up the function of humor as a strategy in dealing with uninvited "civilization." Gene Bluestein, *The Voice of the Folk: Folklore and American Literary Theory* (University of Massachusetts Press, 1972.)

2. 10/13/82. Gordon and Esther Helt at home. To Margaret MacDonald.

3. 1/4/84. Gordon and Esther Helt at home. Margaret Ryan and Margaret MacDonald visiting.

4. 10/13/82. Gordon and Esther Helt at home. To Margaret MacDonald.

5.   10/13/82. Gordon and Esther Helt at home. To Margaret MacDonald.

6.   7/14/85. Murray Read. Sitting by fire on the beach by his home on Guemes Island, Washington, talking with his daughter, Margaret Read MacDonald, about the old days back home in Indiana.

7.   From "Outwitted" by Edwin Markham *in Best Loved Poems of the American People*, ed. by Hazel Feldman (Garden City, NY: Doubleday 1936), p. 67.

8.   Gary B. Melton, citing Roger Barker's "manning theory" suggests that "Undermanned settings need people and are likely to let new residents or visitors remain in anonymity or on the margins of the community." He suggests that this is one factor causing increased friendliness in small communities. There are so few people to accomplish all the work of the community that everyone must be included and encouraged to join in. (Gary B. Melton, "Ruralness as a Psychological Construct" in Allan W. Childs and Gary B. Melton, *Rural Psychology*. (New York: Plenum Press, 1983), pp. 1-13.

Ha! That's I and old Wally.
We had a bunch of fur that time.

We caught that practically all winter.
We had three hundred muskrats...
And I think it was sixty coons...
And five minks...
And I don't know <u>how many</u> foxes...we had
     ten or twelve foxes.

And the coons wasn't worth over a dollar and a half a piece.
Now they're worth forty. (laughs)

That old Wally used to like to trap.
He's a good trapper.

CHAPTER 10
FISH AND FRIENDSHIP

Spiv and Wally Hines are fishing buddies. When I visited in the fall of 1982, they had just discovered the Muskatatuck Refuge over by Seymour. They were going at that fishing pretty hard. Wally would pick Spiv up almost every morning at 6:30 A.M. and off they'd go. Come dragging back about 5 o'clock P.M. with a pail full of perch to clean.

I asked Wally about their friendship. Wally said he had moved into Scipio about 1950 and bought a house from Spiv's sister Pearl. A white frame two-story house just a block up the street from where Spiv lived at the time.

Wally: Course I KNEW Spiv before that.(1)
But then he and I started...I guess our first...escapades together...was trappin'.
He had a little green plywood boat. It was eight foot long.
And he and I dragged that thing...
All OVER this township.
Up and down Sand Creek...

Up and down Wyloose...
We never got to the river in it
   because it was too small.

But that was my first...
Really close relationship with Spiv.
So then we branched out of the trappin'
And then I had that red-bone coon hound...
And we coon hunted.

Then we got into fishin'.
And that...we pretty well quit the trapping because
Well...they got to be so MANY...people trappin'...
That it just took all the fun out of it.
And you run into all kind of people...
I mean not only they'd steal your trap...
But they'd take the FUR.
So we just finally quit...trappin'.

But we've kept up the fishin'
And we have solved many of the world's problems...
Sittin' out in that boat.
I know one time we were sittin'...
In the boat there...
Just above Helt's mill.
And we was trappin' then.
Cold...and rainin'...
I mean it was rainin' STRAIGHT DOWN.
And we was settin' there eatin' our dinner.
Out of...dinner buckets.
And I said to Spiv.
I said, "I sure hope the weather turns off bad...
Because if it does

The furs going to run tonight."
He looked at me and said,
"I don't know how it could get much worse than THIS
    and still be OUTSIDE."

But it WAS an ugly day.

Come wind, come rain, come stormy weather...
It seems like getting out in that boat
    and solving the world's problems
    is always worth the effort to Spiv and Wally.

I commented on how well Spiv and Wally seem to get along.

Wally: Well...we're both...pretty much individualists.
And we never really crossed one another's path.
If we seen that one wasn't exactly satisfied with
    what was being said or goin' on...
We just changed it.
And we've never...never had a word...period.

In the summer of 1952 Wally discovered that the Muskatatuck Refuge just east of Seymour had been opened by the State Fish and Game Department. Wally told about taking Spiv over to the Muskatatuck Refuge for the first time.

Wally: When I retired...I had heard about this...
Refuge...over here...the Muskatatuck Refuge.
I didn't know what was over there...
But a short time before I retired I just drove over there
    to see.

And it was a pretty good sized lake.
So I got to goin' over there...
And was catchin' FISH.
So I asked Spiv one day.
I said, "You wanta go"...I said. "We're goin' fishin'."
He said, "Where're we goin'?"
I said, "I'm gonna take you over to the Refuge."
He said, "I'm not fishin' in no DUCK pond."
I said, "Just wait till you get over there and see what it
    is."

We pulled up there at that lake...
And he said, "Well I never seen...
I didn't know there was anything in here like THAT."

And from that time on...well the rest of that year...
I retired the first of August and it closes October 15.
And I would say that we didn't miss...
very many days a-bein' over there.
From the first of August on until it closed.

Marybelle (Wally's wife speaks up): They opened it and
    closed it.
It opened at sunrise and closed at sunset.
And they'd be gone ALL DAY LONG.

Wally: They open the gates...
You can't stay in there at night.
They open the gates at sunrise.
And we'd be settin' in line.
Or maybe settin' there at the gate...
When they opened it.
So we could get that boat in the water

and get to fishin'.

Fortunately Wally did get sick though one day during my October visit. Otherwise I wouldn't have gotten to interview Spiv at <u>all</u> that trip. My timing was bad since I arrived in early October and the Refuge was due to close for the winter on October 15!

Spiv: Wally's sick today.(2)
I outfished him I reckon.

He's sick today.
Called me at six o'clock...
We had our day...everything lined up for today...
When he called up at six o'clock I said,
"Well, I'd better look...er plan for about three or four
    days ahead now for...maybe a funeral.
Or a lot of sickness or something...
Because whenever a man's sick enough he can't go
    fishin'...
Why he's pretty well GONE.(3)

And that Wally really likes to FISH."

I asked if Spiv would find someone else to go fishing with him.

Spiv: Wally's got the boat.
And he does all the work.
I just go with him.

Hunting and fishing give a man time to think. These activities put space in a life. Space to just sit and relax, or drift off into deep thought, or, with a friend, to talk and talk and talk. In a day of 6 A.M. to 6 P.M. fishing there is plenty of that commodity unknown to city folks...*time*.

The configuration of a conversation changes when there is unlimited time. Time to explore a topic to its end...or freedom to let it drop and just sit in silence...knowing there will always be time down the line to talk again.

Sitting on the edge of a crick waiting for the fish to bite there is time for friendships to deepen. Time to really get to know a friend.

NOTES:
CHAPTER 10

1. Wally Hines at his home. Marybelle Hines, Margaret MacDonald present. 1/3/84.
2. Gordon Helt at his home. 10/12/82.
3. Jens Lund in his fascinating survey of Ohio River Commercial Fisherman speaks of the "singular joys of fishing." "These include the sport of catching fish, the pleasures of being on the river, and the self-respect that comes from managing their own lives and solving the daily puzzle of trying to catch something invisible." He quotes one of his fishermen, Bill Williams, "It's always a challenge out there. Every day it's something new," p. 866. Jens Lund, "Fishing as a Folk Occupation in the Lower Ohio Valley, 2 vols., Ph.D. Indiana University, (January 1983).

Clint Hammon says
"Now that's the biggest one you'll ever <u>catch</u>.
And that's right.
I've never caught one any bigger."

Spiv with 37 and a half pound catfish.

CHAPTER 11
SPIV'S FISH STORIES

The fish story is a favorite Scipio genre. Practically the only genre other than 'dirty joke' to have its own *name*. No one says, "Hey, Spiv, got any good *hunting* stories for us?" Of course Spiv has lots of fish stories to tell. A photo of Spiv with a prize fish hangs on the kitchen wall and he can show you the plaque from the Indianapolis Star Big Fish Contest of 1967. Still his fish stories are most noted for their unusual means of fish catching...rather than their poundage boasts.

Spiv tells about the thirty-seven-and-a-half-pound catfish he caught.

Spiv: I had that dude on a drop line the year BEFORE.(1)
And the crick was real clear.
And there was a grapevine hung out of the L of a tree...
Hung out in the water...
About ten feet from the bank.
I cut it off...so it wouldn't be bothered...
So he wouldn't lap around it...

And the next morning I went down there...
And I seen that old grapevine...
I had this line tied so he couldn't get under the water
    only about a foot.
And when I went down the next morning he was just
    swimmin' in a circle.
Takin' that grapevine way up, you know, past...
Big circle...
That back fin stickin' out of the water...
Comin' around real easy...
I coasted up on the side of him...
And that dirty sucker looked at me...
(Spiv pauses and chuckles, then zips his arms out
    with a loud whooshing sound)
Whoooosh!

There was about ten feet of water underneath of him.
He just snapped that line right square off.

Well...I fished for him all summer...
And didn't catch him.
Now the grapevine had GONE.
But there was this tree that tipped over more in the
    crick...
And I could reach up and get a LIMB.
And I got a small limb and tied it around it...
So it'd be LIMBER, you know.
And I went there the next morning and sure enough...
There in the same place...
That old line was just a-goin' round...
Just like a SUBMARINE.
And I don't know how I'd LAND him.
I had just a little bitty of a NET.

And I just...got down there...
But the water was muddy...
You couldn't see too good, you see.
I just put that net in front of him...
He just swung in there fur as he could GIT.
And I grabbed him by the tail...
Just jerked him like that...
Over in the boat!
And...I got him home.

I met Clint Hammon a-goin' up...
and Clint says,
"Now that's the biggest one you'll ever KETCH."
Spiv chuckles.
And THAT'S RIGHT.
I've never caught one any bigger.

But a couple of years later, Spiv has a catfish tale to top that one.

Spiv: I think I told you about catching that catfish and he tore my minnow bucket up?(2)

Well anyhow...
I'd been a-settin' some lines down there...
Past Bill's over there...
I went down there to go to work...go to look at my lines
    one morning...
And here he sit on the porch.

And I just stopped and said, "Bill, come go with me down to look at my lines."
He said, "Okay wait a minute."

I had my landing net...and everything...
And I'd been a-catchin' some ever mornin'...
Three...or four...
That mornin'...NEVER SCRATCHED A HAIR.

And I said "Now...
'Fore we put our boat in..."
They was a big old holler log layin' there in the water...
Just about six inches under the water...

Oh it was a big one...it was about three foot thick.

We'd looked at our lines down there...
Just I and him in the boat, you see.
And I said, "Well, I'll tell you what's the matter with
    them."
And he said, "What is it?"
And I said, "They're in the hole.
They're a-nestin'."
And it was this time of the year...
And this log...was about...
I suppose it was maybe twice as long as this table.
The water was about that deep and it was just...
It was so big...the water just covered it about THAT
    much.
And they was a big HOLE up here at this top...
About like that...
And then there was one at each end, of course.
But it...the water was deeper down there
And I said to him, I said,
"There's one in that holler log up there where we tied
    our BOAT."
He said, "You reckon?"

And I said, "I bet a hundred dollars there is."

That sucker had a hole in it that BIG.
(The log did.)
Down there where it went through.
Coming past...a limb hung out there...
I just broke me off a twig...about that long...
Stripped it all off...
I run 'er in that little hole here on the top...
Felt in there...
I said, "He's IN THERE, Bill.
LET'S CATCH 'IM."
I just hadn't caught one out of a log...for forty years.

"Naaa," he says...
"Naaa," he says..."Well how will we DO it?"
"Let's get that hook. That last hook we took off of that
    drop line down there...
And we'll tie it onto a STICK
And we'll HOOK 'im."
"OK"
So we went over down there and got that line.
And I got me a good green stick.
So he wouldn't break it off.
'Bout THAT long.
And I tied that old hook right on the end there
    where he wasn't very big...
But it was big enough to hold a fish.
I stuck that back in that...little hole...
I just got 'er back in there...
And I FELT him.

And I said..."I can get him mad..."

(Spiv lowers his voice cautiously as he tells the
    tricky parts that came next)
He never...raised the DEVIL.
Margaret: He bit the stick.
Spiv: Yeah...and I didn't...get him mad.
(Spiv clears his throat. He is being VERY cautious here)
Pulled that out REAL easy
Pulled it right out of that hole.
He was ON there.
Never...raised the dickens or nothin'
He was just as quiet as if I was pullin' a chunk out of
    there.

I just let that stick loose and got both hands down in
    there
And I got 'em in the corner of his MOUTH.
In his gills.
Had to come out through that HOLE...you see.
So when I got him up he was still...
Hadn't done but very little raisin' the Devil.

I got his nose started out of there...
He still didn't raise any dickens and I...
Had a square minnow box in there...about that big...
    that was made out of just FOAM stuff, you know.
And I had some minnows in it. To bait my lines with.
And I had it pretty well full of WATER.
It holds a couple...three gallons.

And you know them old catfish have got horns on the
    side of their head up there and then one right on the
    TOP.
And they all lay back.

When he swims...they lay back.
Well I got that dude started up out of that hole...
And he wouldn't come.
And I looked and...that log was hard.
It wasn't very thick. It was an old hull.
But it was HARD.
And I knocked a piece of hide off the back of my hand...
Blood was just...oh there was blood all over everything.
The water made it bleed MORE you know.
I never turned 'er loose.

But I told Bill, I said "You get the landing net
and stick it over the end of that log back there."
And he got it.
And I figured he'd go...(Spiv makes zipping motion with
     his arm) like that, you know.
And the funny part of it...
I just couldn't keep from thinkin'...
If that fish went out of there.
And Bill kindy overbalance a little bit
     sittin' there holdin' the net like that...
He'd just take Bill right off the back END.
(Spiv laughs at the possibility)
But he didn't go out.

And I brought that dude in.

And I kept a-tellin' Bill, I says
"By golly, Bill, He's a good one."
"How much do you think he is?"
"I don't know, but," I said, "He's a good one."

And I got him right up here...

And BOYS when I started...
I knew better than to fool with that TAIL.
Whenever you fool with that TAIL he's GOIN'
    someplace.
I got him right up.
And as soon as I flipped them HORNS past there...
Gettin' over that hole...
I GIVE him a jerk
Like that (Spiv acts out the jerk)
Course we had the boat right up along the log here...
Right along here.
"HERE!!" (Spiv WHAMS the fish into his imaginary
    boat!)

And MAAAN when he hit that...the inside of the boat
He went crazy.

Just doin' like THAT you know, (Spiv's arm is a
    writhing fish)
He hooked the old FIN...HORN in the side of that box
    up about four or five inches from the bottom...
And I had just three pieces!
Just TORE it all to PIECES.
Three gallon of water in the bottom of that boat
And that crazy fish in there tryin' to ...SWIM.
(Spiv is laughing at the sight)

And we got him up here and he weighed twenty-seven
    pounds and a half.
He was a BIG one.

The fish story is more than just remembrance. This is a
basic genre of storytelling in which every male in the

community participates. This is a matter of *status*. One upmanship here is the name of the game. Spiv's stories, as usual, outdistance everyone else's. Instead of dealing in enormous *size* (though he tells those too), he dwells here on extraordinary ways of *catching* the fish.

Spiv's fish stories are full of incidental information of great value to the young boys or young men around when Spiv is telling his tales, these fishing, hunting, trapping stories act as excellent educational devices. Though I have heard them related mainly in family gatherings where they were offered purely as entertainment it seems likely that Spiv must use these tales also as instructional devices with his young nephews when he is taking them fishing or trapping. Those stories told to me while we were out walking the fields or driving around the country might fall into the same category, as he was specifically trying to educate me about matters of which I had no knowledge. For a different end, of course, I am to put it into a book...not into practice.

NOTES:
CHAPTER 11

1. Gordon Helt at home. To Margaret MacDonald, 7/3/85.
2. Gorden Helt at home to Margaret MacDonald 10/10/87.

Young spiv with catch

CHAPTER 12
THE TRUE STORY, PERSONAL EXPERIENCE, AND IMAGERY

THE TRUTH

Our "fish story" chapter illustrates one of the most notable characteristics of Spiv's storytelling...his insistence that everything he tells be the honest truth. The "fish story" is known for its tendency to lean toward the far side of the truth. and certainly tales of "whoppers" are not unknown in Scipio storytelling. Spiv told me with great delight of the photographs taken up in Wisconsin by Glen Milholland. Glen hung his fish from a tree with a piece of fishing line, then stood way back from it to have his photo taken. The fish appeared gigantic in the photo.(1)

And then...on top of that...
When they cleaned it...
They took a dish pan...
Just turned it upside down...
And laid these...pieces of fish right around the edge of
  it here where they could see it...

And took that.
Just looked like a big dish pan full of fish.
Off of that one fish.
Why they wore that poor old fish OUT.(2)

And yet when Spiv comes to telling his own fish stories, he sticks to the truth. His stories come out as fantastic tales anyway, not because of the gigantic size of this catch...but because of the remarkable means of their capture.(3)

Spiv tells mostly true stories of things that have happened to himself or to friends. He prides himself on "telling it like it is." He does not go in for "stretching the truth." The artistic teller, of course, is always being tugged by the aesthetic impulse to make this the best story possible. The impulse to embellish the tale for aesthetic reasons has to fight the strong moral obligation to keep it the *truth*. Some talkers are known for telling "a lot of baloney." Spiv doesn't want that reputation. He is careful to keep his stories as close to the truth as is artistically possible.(4) "Now, sir, I tell everything that's on the up and up."

Though Spiv is insistent that his stories are all "on the up and up," Scipio uses the word "storytelling" as a synonym for harmless lying. Whenever I ask for "stories" the group jokingly implies that I want to hear some big "lies." Spiv's own stories are jokingly placed in the same genre as the "big story," though everyone agrees that the amazing thing about *Spiv's* storytelling is that it all really did happen.

Jack begins a tale with "You know a good one...that really *happened*..." revealing the implicit understanding that not all stories are the whole truth. Jack, like Spiv, however tells mostly stories which really did happen. The insistence that "stories are close kin to lies" may reflect a tinge of guilt at the way tellers "stretch the truth" rather than suspected story fabrication.(5) Out and out tall tales are not used in this group. Bragging is bad form. The few community tellers who do carry their telling into the realm of out and out lie are well known and their talk taken with a grain of salt.(6) Spiv says of John Andy Day's stories "You couldn't tell when he was lyin' and when he was tellin' the truth."

It is an obvious fact, that *no* story is ever "the truth, the whole truth, and nothing but the truth." Our very perceptions of reality are screened through our own set of past experiences and cultural imperatives. The "true story" must be formulated into a "good story" as well. And with each retelling, its "truth" may change slightly to meet the requirements of the current audience.(7)

The community is well aware of these changes in the truth which inevitably occur. They make allowances for this in their listening. And it is just fine if a story is "improved a little bit" as long as it still "rings true." There is a definite line between the teller who "makes it sound like it could have happened" and the one who "stretches things a bit too far." The audience *wants* to believe that the story they are hearing is really the truth. The aesthetic of the event is damaged if the teller stretches things so far that their trust is broken.(8) This could be seen as a collaboration in the fictionalization of events. The audience knows that they are hearing an elaborated and stylized version of the truth, but choose to accept this. This "told" version often functions better for the group than would an accurate memory of the real event.(9)

Even passing jokes must sound true if Spiv is to pass them on. Spiv tells only jokes which he feels could have really happened. They are thus seen as "true" in a sense. True to *life* at least, and still quite distinct from the out and out lie.(10)

Even when Spiv does tell jokes he usually frames them by saying "That's like the one Mary Monroe told me that time down at the store..." Putting the joke in someone else's repertoire, and clearly labeling it as a "joke," not to be confused with a true story.

Since Spiv prefers to tell only true stories, it follows that his repertoire is built mainly of personal-experience stories, either his own, or those of close friends.

PERSONAL EXPERIENCE AND THE STORYTELLER

Spiv feels that it helps if you know the character you are trying to tell your story about. I asked about his storytelling of Old Bill Little. What does he see in his mind when he tells?

Spiv: I see Old Bill.(11)
I KNOW him you see...
And...if you know what you're TALKING about.
It's a lot easier to TALK about.
You know if you know your CHARACTER...
That you're tellin' your story on.
And you...
And I'm talkin' about KNOW him.
Know how he acts...
Know how he walks...
How he talks...
It's a lot easier DONE.

**And about everything that...I ever think about tellin'...
I'd had a little dealings with SOME way.**

The community seems to acknowledge that "experience" is an important attribute in a storyteller. Jack McConnell began enumerating the general store's prime tellers: "Clark Fitzpatrick...Toot Greathouse...was good. 'Tween Toot makin' up...and what experience he'd *had*...he *was* good. He'd been around a lot. "(12)

As we analyze the way Spiv visualizes his stories we can see why personal experience with the tale event is so important.

HOW SPIV VISUALIZES HIS STORY

Detail

When asked to talk about just what makes Spiv a good storyteller folks usually mention his use of "interesting detail." Perhaps it is because most of Spiv's stories do come from his own personal experience that he can "tell it like it was."

My father, Murray Read, says of Spiv:

**"He goes into all the details...about it...(13)
But the details aren't TIRING.
He wants you to get the straight picture.
Of how it REALLY happened. You know.
And that's the way Gordon DOES it.
Everything in detail.
But it's not a detail that's TIRING to you.
You ENJOY it.
Yeah.
So he's a good STORY teller."**

The detail referred to here is a detail of place, circumstance and characterization, not a visually descriptive detail.

Reliving the Scene

In his retelling of personal experience stories, Spiv seems to be reliving his scenes...but he seems to be *re-feeling* them rather than reseeing them. In his story of catching the big catfish with the stick he is careful to explain every action. He appears to be reliving the entire episode as he recounts the tale. When he finally gets the fish on the end of the stick, Spiv clears his throat nervously and positions himself to *ease* the fish out of the log. It's as if he is feeling again the nervous tension and tentative nature of the moment he is describing. The descriptive material Spiv provides in this tale functions more as stage direction and an indicator of how things *felt* than of how things looked. He tells us exactly how thick and how long the hollow log was and how deep in the water. He tells us the length of his twig. Where the hole in the log was, and where he tied his hook. He describes the   flimsiness of the foam minnow box, and the hardness of the hollow log hull. The only truly visual part of the entire episode is "blood all over everything."

Thought Processes

Though visual detail is not basic to Spiv's remembrance, his own thought processes during the adventure *are* important. Spiv spends considerable attention on his hunch that the big catfish might be lying up in the hollow log. He shows how he "felt in there" for the fish, notes his feelings that he hadn't caught a fish out of a log like that for forty years. Spiv explains to his partner how he'll hook the fish, chooses just the right green stick, reaches in "and I *felt* him." Spiv thinks "I can get him mad," but he eases him up, then he realizes that he "had to come out through that *hole*," then he sees how hard the log is and realizes he can't knock the hole any bigger. Spiv thinks to himself that the fish is going to bolt any minute so he tells Bill to put the net over the back of the log. Then he has to laugh at himself, thinking that if the fish does bolt it will pull Bill right off the end of the log into the water. Spiv eases the fish out of the hole...but "I knew better than to fool with that tail."

The whole story is told from the point of view of inside Spiv's head. We know exactly what he is thinking at each step of the way and it is in Spiv's thought processes that the real drama lies. The real story here is in just what was going through Spiv's mind while he was catching the fish.

Stage Directions

Describing the setting is a *literary* art. Spiv's storytelling is a *theater* art. Characterization, motivation, dialogue, action and staging are the basics.

Spiv uses very little description. There is nothing of the colorful descriptive passage in his stories, but he is very concerned with stage directions. He makes it clear where everyone is standing or sitting...what their motions are...even acting these out at times. He shows what noises occurred, imitating these.

It is unimportant to paint full sets for his stories...they are dramatic pieces which play just fine on a bare stage. Elaborately described settings are unnecessary and would in fact *detract* from the story. Spiv's old-codger stories illustrate this.

In the story of Old Bill Little and the cats we have no description of Bill Little, the cats, or the room. We *are*, however, given explicit stage directions for the action that follows. Wiggle Emly sits in a straight-back chair leaning against the wall. He reaches behind himself and scratches on the wallpaper. The cats come swarming about the door outside. Old Bill Little grabs the broom, runs to the door, and BATS cats.

In the auction scene, again no descriptive passages are included to tell us how the auction looked. But the stage directions are explicit. Bill Little is on the opposite side of the crowd from Spiv. The auctioneer, of course, is understood to be in the middle, somewhere between the two.

In the story of Old John Kane stepping them off...we are given no information about what the garage looked like, or Old John Kane, or Dally. But again stage directions are clear. Dally is lying under a car...the wide door to the garage is open...Old John Kane is strutting past the open door calling in to Dally under the car.

Characterization and Motivation

Though the descriptive mode is not compatible with these tales, emphasis on characterization is vital.

The Old Codger stories, of course, center on the idea of a character. The entire story is told as an illustration of the subject's unusual character.

But Spiv takes pains to paint a picture of the character of the Old Codger's tormentors too.

He begins the story of Old Bill Little and the cats by telling about the prank's perpetrator Wiggle Emly. "But Wiggle...He's seventy-seven years old now. And he was a pistol. He'd devil you or devil somebody else REGARDLESS."

Of Old Bill Little he says merely, "He was an ODDITY." The story will tell the rest.

Spiv is careful to show the motivation for the incident..."They was a-sittin' there, you know...thinkin' of something to talk about...and pass the time away in the evening...and Wiggle...he happened to think..." Their mental frame is shown...they are bored, trying to think of something to talk about...Wiggle gets a bright idea!

Uncle Earnest...who told Spiv the story gets a character comment too..."Uncle Earnest was settin' up with...Uncle Earnest knew well enough what was goin' on, you know...he'd have to laugh regardless."

In the Old John Kane story we get a glimpse at Dally's character as well as Old John Kane's. "Old Dally's tellin' me about it and he'd just bust out..."

Visual Imagery and Spatial Imagery

Much has been written about the strong visual imagery of the master storyteller. The master teller is one who can "make you picture it" as the story is told. Because of this skill, the teller is assumed to possess a complete picture in the mind as well.(14) Examination of Spiv's tale texts raises some suspicion about this assumption. The quality of the mind "picture" deserves some consideration.

The notion of a "picture" in the mind is perhaps misleading to begin with. Psychologists point out that "pictures" are not the equivalent of photographs to be pulled out at any point in time and scanned for detail and interpreted.(15) They are, instead, mental images which have already been interpreted and organized. What is *remembered* is a version of reality restructured to fit our individual expectations.

The research on memory and mental imagery is extensive and inconclusive.(16) People appear to have different learning preferences, some prefer visual cues, some verbal. And no two individuals "picture" a thing in quite the same way.

It seems clear that Spiv "sees" his stories in terms of action, spatial relationships, and sound. When asked what he sees when he tells about Old Bill Little, Spiv declares, "I see Old Bill. I *know* him you see. ...And I'm talkin' about *know* him. Know how he acts...Know how he walks...How he talks..."

Notice that Spiv does not mention knowing what Old Bill *looks* like. It is a storyteller's job (as is the actor's) to re-create Old Bill Little through movement (or reported movement) and dialogue. Spiv remembers also exactly where everyone stood in the episodes he relates, but his memory for specific visual detail seems unimportant to his art.

This is not surprising since the memory for spatial relationships seems much stronger than memory for visual detail. Think back to the most recent time you were in an unfamiliar setting. Can you remember where you stood in that room? Where other people were in relation to you? Where you were in relation to the walls, the furniture? Probably. Can you recall the pattern on the rug? The color of the walls? Describe the objects on the tabletops in the room? Probably not. Usually such details cannot be accessed in memory unless they figure in the story you have to tell of that event. Only if you make a mental note of specific details at the time can they be recalled later.

However, while it is possible to walk through a room without noticing the color of the walls, the *placement* of the walls in relation to your body is taken into account without conscious thought. This is basic information necessary to propel ourselves through space without colliding with objects. This may be one of the most constant bits of data we solicit from our environment. It is not surprising then that spatial relationships are remembered and play an important part in personal narrative.

One interesting point to note in this discussion of visual imagery is the fact that the teller's ability to create detailed imagery in the listener's mind is not necessarily tied to the detail of his own internal imagery.(17) It is the listener who supplies most of the detail. Some paint lavish pictures around the story they hear, others "see" mainly motivation and action as they listen.(18)

Auditory Imagery

We see that Spiv formulates his stories through spatial imagery as well as visual imagery. Action, characterization, and motivation seem more basic than visual descriptors in his tellings. It is possible too that auditory imagery is crucial in Spiv's retellings, memory not only of the tale-making event's language, but also of his own former tellings as formed into spoken word. In this context it may be interesting to look at Spiv's use of conversation in story and at the stability of text in his tales through repeated tellings.

DIALOGUE

Dialogue is a favorite device in Spiv's tellings. He reproduces the humorous conversations which took place in his tale-events verbatim...Spiv at least believes this to be so. He makes much use of mimicry and dramatic intonation. The humor of his tales often lies in quoted speeches.

The story of Old Bill Little and the cats is all silent action in Spiv's telling. But the humor isn't complete until Spiv adds Wiggle's comment, "They *always* do that" "Ever time somebody dies they *always* do that!"

The humor of Old Bill Little's trouble with his newly bought car lies mainly in his directions to Dally as reported by Spiv (who heard this from Dally)..."Dally," he says... "Dally, I want you to work on that *car* there." "Now," he says, "the *trouble*...the trouble is right *there*." And he stuck his finger in that fan while the motor was runnin'. He said, "the trouble's right in *there*. That cut a *finger* off."

Spiv uses dialogue also to enliven his stories, steer us away from straight monologue, and lend it an air of verisimilitude. In one of Spiv's fish stories the scene really comes to life for us as Spiv and Bill mutter about whether or not there is a big fish lying around there.

Spiv: There's one in that holler log up there where we
    tied our boat.
Bill: You reckon?
Spiv: I bet a hundred dollars there is.

In Spiv's narration, Bill acts as Spiv's straight man and through his questions enables Spiv to explain his own assessment of the situation.

Bill: Well, how will we do it?
Spiv: Let's take that hook...

Spiv: By golly Bill. He's a good one.
Bill: How much do you think he is?
Spiv: I don't know, but--He's a good one.

Spiv: Well I'll tell you what's the matter with them.
Bill: What is it?
Spiv: They're in the hole. They're a-nestin'.

STABILITY OF LANGUAGE THROUGH REPEATED TELLINGS

Spiv's stories remain consistent in text through repeated tellings collected over a period of years.(19)

If Spiv were recreating his story each time from a remembered visual image, his text would show more variation. It seems more likely that he is remembering the aural image of his previous tellings. Not just the actions and the motivations are the same in Spiv's repeated tales, but the words he uses, and the very tone of voice are identical. Spiv is reproducing a learned piece.

Each successive telling brings back a memory, not only of the actual event which spawned the story, but also of the language in which the story was previously told. With time the "truth" becomes the story rather than the actual event and access to memories of the event itself are blocked by the "story" which has superseded it.

The repeated insistence that one's stories are "the truth" is important in maintaining one's status in the community as a "truthful" teller. But this insistence may also reveal a psychological anxiety over the elusive nature of memory. He insists that this story is true, wanting to believe that his memory is accurate. But, as we have seen, the material available to us for the creation of our personal narratives is fragmentary at best.

NOTES
CHAPTER 12

1. Roger Welsch discusses prank photography in *Tall Tale Postcards: A Pictorial History* (South Brunswick: A.S. Barnes, 1976).
2. 7/3/82. Spiv Helt to Margaret MacDonald looking at photos.
3. Spiv's stories resemble Stith Thompson *motif X1153 Lie: person catches fish by remarkable trick*, though since these are no lies perhaps they would best be classified with *H1154.4 Task: catching huge fish without nets or tackle*. Stith Thompson, *Motif-Index of Folk-Literature*. (Bloomington and London: Indiana University Press, 1966).
4. The importance of keeping personal narrative within an aura of "truth" has been discussed by several folklorists. See Richard Bauman, "The La Have Island General Store: Sociability and Verbal Art in a Nova Scotia Community" *Journal of American Folklore* 85, no. 338, (Oct-Dec. 1972): 330-343. See pp. 334-335; Michael Taft, "An Evening of Storytelling" in his *Discovering Saskatchewan Folklore: Three Case Studies*, (Edmonton; NeWest Press, n.d.), pp. 45-82; Bauman, Richard, "Any Man Who Keeps More'n One Hound'll Lie to You: Dog Trading and Storytelling at Canton, Texas" in *And Other Neighborly Names: Social Process and Cultural Image in Texas Folklore*, edited by Richard Bauman and Roger D. Abrahams, (Austin and London; The University of Texas Press, 1981), pp. 74-103. However, in "Any Man Who Keeps More'n One Hound'll Lie to You," (p.90) Bauman notes: "The aesthetic considerations of artistic performance may demand the embellishment or manipulation--if not the sacrifice--of the literal truth in the interests of greater dynamic tension, formal elegance, surprise value, contrast, or other elements which contribute to excellence in performance in this subculture."
5. Richard Bauman's discussion of Texas hound dog traders is helpful here. "The interesting and noteworthy thing about the sociable storytelling of hound-dog men is that, although it is strongly recognized as susceptible to lying, the lying is overwhelmingly licensed as part of the fundamental ethos of sociability. That is, by not challenging the truthfulness of another's stories, one may reasonably

expect to be accorded the same license in presenting one's own image-building narratives and crafting one's own artful performances. Then too, it is only susceptibility we are talking about; not every personal narrative about dogs and hunting involves lying, nor is it always clear or consciously recognized which do and which do not. There is merely a persistent sense that every story might." ("Any Man Who Keeps More'n One Hound'll Lie to You," p. 91).

6.   Henry Glassie's Ballymenone folk seem to value qualities similar to those in Spiv's Scipio. Hugh Nalon says "There bes a class of men and they go in for tellin stories, but there bes a kind of flow--they make themselves very bright, do ye know, without anyone waitin for to pass that judgment; you know what I mean? That they come out *bright.* Och, they're always the winner in their stories. Anybody that was always talkin on their own, their own abilities or their own smartness, do ye know, they were always braggin of himself, do ye know. He wasn't well thought of; the man that come out bright in all, in every transaction. The man that would get into where he failed himself, that man was thought the honestest man and the best company. Aye. There was give and take in that man," p. 38. Henry Glassie, *Passing the Time in Ballymenone: Culture and History of an Ulster Community.* (Philadelphia: University of Pennsylvania Press, 1982).

Sandra Stahl notes that "Audiences will tolerate embellishments that bring the story closer to thematic or stylistic perfection, but they are unwilling to accept a person's own testimony if his actions seem too obviously exemplary," p. 119. Sandra K.D. Stahl, "The Personal Narrative as a Folklore Genre," (Ph.D. diss., Indiana University, 1975).

7.   Sandra Stahl suggests these three points and provides an excellent discussion of the truth-falsehood question in "The Personal Narrative as a Folklore Genre" Ph.D., Indiana University, 1975. "This relatively minor degree of falsification occurs at three levels: first, in the teller's perception of the experience; second, in the initial telling of the personal narrative; and third, in the re-adaptations of the story to the varying contexts of retelling." (p. 115).

8.   Richard Bauman finds a similar approach in his Newfoundland community. "A corollary of the personal nature of the yarns was that they were told and accepted as essentially true. ...Still, it was commonly recognized that storytellers tend to embellish their yarns for greater personal effect"..."They'd tell a story tonight and a week from tonight it would be a little better. The core of truth was insisted upon, however"--"They weren't really lyin' about their stories; after a while

they just got polished up a bit." "Maybe somebody would add a little bit onto it--make it sound better--but most of it was true." Those few storytellers who went beyond the limits of creative license to complete distortion or fabrication were singled out for gentle ridicule and not taken very seriously. Every one knew who they were." (pp. 335-336) Richard Bauman, "The La Have Island General Store: Sociability and Verbal Art in a Nova Scotia Community" *Journal of American Folklore* 85 (1972), pp. 331-343.

9.   Sandra Stahl: "It would seem in fact that a degree of fantasy or falsification may positively effect the credibility of the story by increasing the familiarity or universality of the experience for both the teller and his listeners." (p. 115). Sandra K.D. Stahl, "The Personal Narrative as a Folklore Genre" (Ph.D. diss., Indiana University, 1975).

10.   Robert Adams says of another Indiana teller, "Sullivan views most of his jokes and stories as bits of rarefied reality, if not true, then at least illustrative of general truths." (p. 42) Robert J. Adams, "Raconteur and Repertoire: A Study of a Southern Indiana Storyteller and his Material," M.A., Indiana University, 1966.

Elliot Oring's research on chizbat humor might have been written of the Scipio humorous anecdote. Of this Israeli joking form his informants said: "A chizbat is a word that covers actual stories with a little bit of fixing corners. A story that happened, but a little bit imagination. But the imagination in this case is just to make the story a little better; not to change the story. It is not a lie but fixed truth." (p. 360) Oring deduces that "what is meant by truth is not primarily related to any level of historical reality but rather to some a-historical metaphorical realm." He cites another informant, Dan Ben-Amos, on the transformation of jokes to chizbat. "You felt by the smell it was essentially a joke...It is possible that occasional jokes sneaked into the corpus of chizbat, that were worked into chizbat, but for us it didn't matter because it acquired a whole new value." Elliot Oring, "Hey, You've Got No Character: Chizbat Humor and the Boundaries of Israeli Identity", *Journal of American Folklore*, 86, no. 342, (Oct-Dec. 1973): 358-366.

11.   Spiv Helt. 7/3/85.

12.   Jack McConnell. 7/3/85.

13.   Murray Read. 1/28/85.

14.   Folklorist Richard S. Tallman stresses the importance of visual imagery in "You Can Almost Picture It: The Aesthetic of a Nova Scotia Storyteller" in *Folklore Forum*, 197, pp. 121-130. "...the story itself

becomes a visual drama in the mind's eye of both the teller and his audience. The extent to which a story is appreciated by any one person thus depends upon the associations and connotations that the story calls to mind. The more vivid and detailed the mind picture is, the better the story." Tallman concludes that "at the core of the aesthetic of all folk narrative is an appreciation of the imagery of the narrative, a sense that 'you can almost picture it' as the story is told."

15. Pylyshyn, Z.W. "What the mind's eye tells the mind's brain: A critique of mental imagery." *Psychological Bulletin*, 80, no. 1-24, (1973); or for an introduction to learning and memory theory, see Arthur Wingfield, *Human Learning and Memory: An Introduction.* (New York: Harper & Row, 1979).

16. For literature reviews see John T.C. Richardson, *Mental Imagery and Human Memory.* (London: The Macmillan Press Ltd., 1980); Geir Kaufmann, *Visual imagery and Its Relation to Problem Solving: A Theoretical and Experimental Inquiry.* (Bergen: Universitetsforlaget, 1979). Sydney Joelson Segal, Editor, *Imagery: Current Cognitive Approaches.* (New York and London: Academic Press, 1971).

17. Professional storyteller Jay O'Callahan in his master class video tape on storytelling speaks of the importance of creating strong visual imagery for the audience. He proceeds to illustrate this by telling a brief story lacking entirely in descriptive matter. When questioned about this he explains that he cuts his stories back to a sparse narration of events in order to allow the audience plenty of spaces between his words to create their *own* pictures. Guide to "Jay O'Callahan: A Master Class in Storytelling." West Tisbury, Mass.: Vineyard Video Productions 1983.

18. I asked my twelve year old daughter to describe what she "saw" when I told her a story. She related an elaborate description of the interior of a home in which one story occurs. She described the furnishings down to the objects on the mantelpiece, and even explained the floor plan of the house, including unseen rooms. In my rendition of the story I mention nothing about the house except that it has a mantelpiece, a cupboard and a door.

When I asked my ten year old daughter what *she* saw in the story, she grabbed a pencil and paper and began to draw stick figures and arrows to show where they *moved* as the story progressed. Her imagery seemed tied to space and motion within the tale. I, myself, "see" very little more than shadowy conceptual motion as I tell, the *sound* of the language in which I have couched the tale previously seems to be the thread which guides me.

19. Sandra Stahl discusses this stability of repeated tellings in "The Personal Narrative as a Folklore Genre" (Ph.D. diss., Indiana University, 1975), pp. 109-110; and Marjorie Bennett shows stability in texts collected over a period of years from her Washington cowboy/logger informant Dell Ringer. "Individual and Community in Personal narratives of Storyteller Del Ringer of North Bend, Washington," by Marjorie Bangs Bennett (Ph.D. diss., University of Washington, 1986).

Spiv tells Photographer about catching the 32 and 1/2
pound catfish. Photo by Denny Morrow

CHAPTER 13
DEFINING THE MASTER TELLER

Is Spiv a "master teller"? The community seems to think so. When I mentioned down at the Scipio store that I was trying to collect stories around Scipio, Jeanette told me right off "Well you'd better talk to Spiv Helt up here." I asked Spiv's nephew Gerald who some of the better storytellers around here are. "Well, *Spiv's* one of the *best*." When I asked my father for stories about Scipio he told me, "Spiv's the *story* teller. He's the one you ought to be talking to."

My parents were lifelong friends of Spiv and Esther. We spent many a Saturday night out at their house when I was growing up, eating popcorn and apples and visiting. They owned a TV set years before we broke down and bought one, and for a while we made regular Saturday night pilgrimages to Scipio to watch wrestling matches on TV. I asked my father just what makes Spiv such a good storyteller.

Murray: Because he tells his stories in an interesting WAY.(1)

That interests PEOPLE.
And his stories always...whatever he TELLS...is
**   INTERESTING.**
And...don't make any difference what the story IS or is
**   ABOUT...**
Spiv tells it in a way...that everybody just LISTENS.
And they listen...and they ENJOY it.

Murray begins to elaborate ways in which Spiv is a good teller. Let's look at Murray's critique along with comments of Spiv and other Scipio folks, as we try to understand the master teller as defined by the community itself. The teller good enough to be singled out as one who "can really tell them" might exhibit several of the following qualities.

WIDE PERSONAL EXPERIENCE

As we saw in Chapter 12, a host of interesting life experiences is one of the qualities attributed to prize storytellers.(2)

When I asked Jack McConnell about good storytellers he'd heard, he named several.

"Toot Greathouse...was good.(3)
Tween Toot makin' up...and what experience he'd
HAD...
He WAS good.
He'd been around a lot."

When I asked Gerald if he told stories like Spiv, he said no. "I haven't had all the experience he'd had I *guess*. Or don't *remember* them probably."(4)

GOOD MEMORY

Coupled with wide experience one needs, of course, a good memory. Other Scipio folks may have had plenty of storyable experiences but don't remember them now. Of course the person who thinks of himself as a storyteller is much more apt to remember a good story, since he is formulating the anecdote as it occurs and in the process giving it a fixed form for memory retrieval.

LARGE REPERTOIRE

Spiv says of one of his favorite tellers, Clark Fitzpatrick, "He had a new one to tell every time he met ye." Murray says of Spiv that, "He never tells the same story twice." My tapes reveal this not to be exactly so, but Spiv's repertoire *is* vast, and constantly building.(5)

Repertoire size is related to wide personal experience and good memory. And a large repertoire is one of the factors which allows the teller to slip an appropriate tale into almost any conversation.

SPECIALIZED REPERTOIRE

The master teller keeps a mental "file" of stories on hand...ready to tell to certain individuals. Certain tales are put aside for specific audiences. Esther says of the Kentucky Switchblade "I'll have to show that to Lillie. She'll get a big kick out of that." As Lillie is from Kentucky, all Kentuckian jokes are kept in mind until they can be related to her.

Spiv and "Buckle," the barber, regularly exchange humorous anecdotes about the infirmities of old age, and the problems of 'controlling' the wife. When Spiv runs over his wife Esther's foot with the wheelbarrow, he formats this into a humorous story to tell Buckle.

IDENTIFICATION WITH THE TALE

Margaret: Seems like he could make almost ANYTHING interesting though.
Murray: Yes he CAN.
Because he tells it in a WAY...that...
Murray's wife Jane jumps in: Well you see...what you
      DO...is put yourSELF into it.
You know he FEELS it.
He makes YOU feel it.
Margaret: Yes he does.

As we saw in our discussion of Spiv's imagery in Chapter 13 he does "feel" his stories. The mental processes of his characters are in the forefront of most of his tales.

ENJOYS THE TALE

Jane: You know if YOU...think it's funny...why you're
      gonna tell it in the right way.
      Jane gives an example of a friend of hers who told a
joke. "And you know it was funnier to hear him TELL
it...because he got such a kick out of it."

Spiv's enjoyment of the tale enhances it. As Jane points out, if *you* think it's funny, you're going to tell it in the right way. You like the stories with which you have a rapport.

And stories which are meaningful to you are the ones you can interpret best for your audience. Spiv is good at identifying story material which he can get a kick out of.

Ability to Capitalize on Humor in Tale

Spiv is also very good at retelling to capitalize on the humor involved.

Murray: Well so often...the way things are told...they're
     funnier than when they actually happened.
It's the way it's TOLD.
And uh that's uh...Spiv's secret.

This tendency to create a humorous narrative out of seemingly non-humorous events was discussed in the chapter on "Self-Talk in Scipio."

Murray: Now Spiv...he don't tell stories with the
purpose...of ENTERTAINING you.
You know...He don't TELL a story that way.
He's not tellin' it with the IDEA...of makin' you laugh...
     or entertaining you...
He just tells you because...they just come to his head...
     and they're just OUT.
He just TELLS them.
And they just fit right in with the CONVERSATION.
And that's the way his stories EVOLVE.
That's what makes them so GOOD.

The tale is best accepted if it appears to "fit in with the conversation."(6) Making the story appear relevant to the matter at hand is important.

Humility is a prime quality in Scipio. Folks who *think* they are clever are not appreciated. Some storytellers are obviously *trying* to be funny. A story can be spoiled if the teller's ego is so big that it overshadows his tale.(7) Spiv's storytelling is appreciated because he isn't telling it to show how funny he is. He just tells it, and it *is* funny and you split your sides laughing.

TALE ORGANIZATION

Little is said about the skill of organizing a tale. But "getting it straight" is probably the most important skill of all. When asked for advice on storytelling, Spiv says "Tell it like it is and don't back-track" and "make it plain." His complaint that "Some fellows will leave out 95% of it and you have to make up the rest for yourself" probably refers partially to an inability to organize the plot.

USE OF DETAILS

Murray: He goes into all the details...about it...but the details aren't tiring.
He wants you to get the straight picture.
Of how it REALLY happened, you know.

And that's the way Spiv DOES it.
Everything in detail.
But it's not a detail that's TIRING to you.
You ENJOY it.
So he's a good STORY teller.

When I asked Spiv's nephew Gerald what made Spiv such a good storyteller, he mentioned the same thing.

Gerald: Oooohhh DETAILS I guess.(8)
He gets all the details.

While Spiv is known for the fascinating detail in his stories, his own criteria recommend that you "Don't stretch anything when you're tellin' but make it plain."(9) The ability to elaborate must be a prime quality for the master teller, but it shouldn't *sound* like you are stretching it out. As Murray says, "Spiv puts in a lot of detail. But it's not the detail that's *tiring*." This is because Spiv's detail is *pertinent*. He doesn't appear to be stretching it out. On the other hand, he makes sure all important detail is *in* there.

"Some fellows will leave out 95% of it and you have to make up the rest for yourself,"(10) says Spiv. He praises Eunice Carmichael's telling about her plane trip to California.

"She never left a move out.
From the time she left.
Till she got back."(11)

Spiv's criteria may be similar to that of another fine folk narrator, Abraham Lincoln. Of Lincoln's style, folklorist Richard Dorson says, "the narrative possesses enough detail to depict the scene and engage the listener's interest but avoids extraneous description that could overload the story and smother the moral. As Horace Porter said, Lincoln's tale was neither too broad nor too long."(12)

In Chapter 12, we noted the *kinds* of detail Spiv is fond of. Thought process, characterization, stage directions, dialogue, as well as plot must be detailed. Descriptive visual imagery other than the purely spatial seems less important.

THE ABILITY TO RELATE THIS TALE TO THE EXPERIENCE OF THE AUDIENCE

**Murray: And they relate...because you're close enough
    and you KNOW the people...
You KNOW them.
So you can RELATE to them.
And that's one reason that...
Storytelling is interesting if you can relate to the
    STORY.
Now if you was to happen to tell a story...about
    something so foreign...to people's knowledge...
It's not interesting.**

**You've gotta tell something to people...
they're interested...
because they KNOW...what you're talking ABOUT.**

**And that...that was SPIV.
These stories and the people that he would tell...
    was people that you KNOW about...HEARD
    about...and all...,you know.
That's why they're INTERESTING.
Because they relate to YOU.
And you can relate to THEM.**

It is true that Spiv does always make his stories relate to the local situation. Even when he tells a passing joke, he frames it so that it sounds as if it took place right around here. And most of his repertoire is local anecdote concerning places and people that everyone in the audience is familiar with.

In our discussion of the New Year's Eve 1985 storytelling texts we noted the importance of fixing both place and person before beginning a Scipio narrative. This is one technique which helps relate the tale to the audience's experience. Each tale is local and therefore meaningful.

But it is more than just topic which makes Spiv's tellings so good. It's the *way* he tells it, and the way Spiv relates to his tale.

RAPPORT WITH AUDIENCE

As Murray says, when Spiv talks...he "tells it in a way...that everybody just listens."..."and they *enjoy* it." He has the ability to draw people to him and to tell stories in a way "that interests people." Aspects of rapport are discussed more fully in Chapter 4. This undoubtedly is a primary quality for the master teller.

OPPORTUNITY TO PRACTICE

I asked Spiv how he got to be such a good storyteller. "I just told so many I got in practice, I reckon."(13)

Storytelling thrives where there is a chance to practice.(14) Scipio's lifestyle makes time for this. Spiv, Crescent Miller, Frank McConnell and their wives used to get together regularly to play cards and visit. Those families went off to Wisconsin for fishing trips at least once a year, all of them piling into two or three cabins at one of their favorite lakes up there. And of course Crescent ran the garage and Frank the local store, both centers of storytelling

activity in the community. Frank's son, Jack, is quite a
storyteller today, as we have seen.

Murray comments on the practice of storytelling in
Scipio and moves on to another topic, the importance of
relating the tale to the experience of the audience.

**Margaret: There seem to be a lot of good stories out
there around Scipio.**
Murray: Well...there are.
And one reason I think there ARE.
Is because they TELL stories.
Now Jack McConnell...is a good storyteller.
And those fellows out there...they get together a lot.
And they TALK a lot.
And they relate their experiences...and all.

THE SOCIAL IDENTITY OF THE STORYTELLER

Some of the qualities mentioned here by Spiv and his
listeners have been discussed in previous chapters. But we
discover several points which our discussions of teller style
(chapter 4) and imagery (chapter 12) did not reach. Here we
find more emphasis on the teller as an individual. What is it
about Spiv as a *person* that makes him a good teller?

The attitude of the teller emerges as important here.
Spiv is funny because he doesn't appear to be "trying to
make you laugh." He is a good teller because he *enjoys* his
tale. Spiv's telling style is certainly not the only one which
pleases audiences in Scipio. But any teller who achieves
repeated success must have a personality which wins the
audience. Spiv relates his stories to the experience of his
audience. He seems to care about his audience. "He *wants*
you to get the straight picture," says Murray.

The teller's background is also important. He must be in a situation which allows him lots of opportunity to practice. And he must have had opportunity to hear other master tellers perform.

Another important quality which emerges from this discussion is the value placed on repertoire size. The true master teller can "tell a new one every time he sees you." Prodigious memory as well as skill at applying tales to the situation are implied.

These points relate to the phenomenon Robert Adams calls "the social identity of a storyteller." We have seen that many Scipio tellers use a style similar to Spiv's in their telling. And their performance, while perhaps not as intriguing as Spiv's, is far from incompetent. With a little practice and the right audience most of Scipio's tellers could shine.(15) The master teller differs from others not so much in style as in attitude: master tellers have begun to think of themselves as "storytellers." The "social identity" of "storyteller" has been assumed.

To reach this point a young person probably passes years listening to older tellers. Since everyone tells stories everytime they talk, there is always opportunity to practice this art. In Scipio the well-told story is an appreciated art form. One not only tells stories, but one tells them within an aesthetically critical context. A good teller is appreciated. Experience in this environment naturally hones one's skills.

Gradually certain individuals begin to get a reputation for being good storytellers. Once they begin to see themselves as good storytellers the die is cast. They are now on the lookout for story material. They are constantly restructuring their experiences into narratives suitable for telling. They learn to "look for the funny side of things."

And as we have mentioned, now that they are making a point of structuring reality into story, their adventures become easier to recall.

As they tell repeatedly their performative skills sharpen as well, and they learn how to play with the audience, how to interpret the tale for the audience's clear understanding and enjoyment, and how to caretake the audience, leading them skillfully through a rewarding experience of "group play" in the story event.

The master teller now assumes a personal *responsibility* for the experience of the audience. At this point the "social identity of storyteller" has clearly been assumed by this individual. The community will now *expect* story performance, request it, and reward it.

The community has *acquired* a storyteller, and will probably not let him get away. Note that the community's role in the creation of this teller is far from passive. The community desires and needs a few good tellers on hand. It tends to pick favorite young tellers and groom them, through constant reinforcement and opportunity for repeated tellings. It is the community, in a sense, that can be said to have "made" this teller.

Drawing from our discussion in this chapter, and Chapters 4 and 12, we might suggest criteria for the master storyteller in Scipio. Not all of these criteria need apply to every teller. But each criteria has been seen to be prized in *some* Scipio teller.

*   *   *

CRITERIA FOR THE MASTER TELLER
* * *

A. TELLER AND REPERTOIRE: EXPERIENCE/ REPERTOIRE/ PROGRAMMING

- The master teller may be noted for wide experience.
- The master teller will have a remarkable memory.
- Experience plus memory yield a large repertoire of tales.
- The master teller is skilled in fitting the tale to the conversational context or selecting the right tale for the moment. A large repertoire is one ingredient necessary to this art.

B. TELLER'S RELATIONSHIP TO THE TALE: IDENTIFIES WITH TALE/ ENJOYS TALE/ INTERPRETS TALE

- The master teller identifies with the tale.
- The master teller enjoys the tale and the telling.
- Because the teller identifies with the tale and enjoys it, the teller is able to *interpret* the tale for the audience.

C. TELLER AND TEXT:ORGANIZES, USES DETAIL, PERSONALIZES, CAPITALIZES ON HUMOR

- The master teller can organize a tale text well.
- The master teller will put in just the right detail.
- The master teller will relate the tale to the experience of the audience.
- The master teller will capitalize on the humorous possibilities of the tale.

D. TELLER AND PERFORMANCE

- The master teller is skilled in the use of voice and gesture.
- The master teller is skilled in effective delivery (pacing and pause, rhythm, parallel form).
- The master teller will "frame" the tale a appropriately through introductory remarks and tale capping.

E. TELLER AND AUDIENCE: CREATES RAPPORT/ CARE-TAKES

- . The master teller will create a rapport with the audience.
- The master teller will care-take the audience through performative skills.
- The master teller will choose the right tale for this audience and relate the tale to the audience's experience.

F. WHAT MAKES A MASTER TELLER? ROLE MODEL/ PRACTICE/ SOCIAL IDENTITY

- The master teller will have had opportunity to hear other master tellers.
- The master teller will have had opportunity to practice.
- The master teller will have a personality which pleases his audience.
- The master teller will have received reinforcement from a caring audience.
- The master teller will assume the 'social identity' of the storyteller.

CHAPTER 13

1. Murray Read and his wife Jane, Guemes Island, Washington. Margaret MacDonald and Murray's sister, Sally Read Johnston present. All Murray's quotes in this chapter are from this session. Though Murray now lives in Washington State, he spent the first 72 years of his life in Jennings County and it seems fair to accept his comments as 'in-group' criteria for Spiv's storytelling.

2. Richard Tallman drew the same conclusions from his informant, Bob Coffil. "Coffil's initial definition of a good storyteller is someone who has traveled in his work and has experiences to tell about that the stay-at-home lacks," p. 125. Richard S. Tallman, "You Can Almost Picture It: The Aesthetic of a Nova Scotia Storyteller." *Folklore Forum.* 197, pp. 121-130.

Richard Bauman says of his La Have Island Storytellers "When I asked what made a good talker or a good storyteller, the answer... was that the older men with the widest range of experience were the best talkers and storytellers," (p. 340). His informant tells him "The ones who traveled the most could tell the most and best"..."The men that went to Labrador---how they lived there in amongst those people---that would be quite a story," (pp. 334-335). Richard Bauman, "The La Have Island General Store: Sociability and Verbal Art in a Nova Scotia Community" *Journal of American Folklore* 85, No. 338, (Oct-Dec. 1972): 330-343.

3. 7/3/85. Jack McConnell to Margaret MacDonald. At Gordon Helt's home, Esther and Ledell McConnell also present.

4. 7/2/85. Gerald Helt. At Pert Helt's home. To Margaret MacDonald.

5. A seemingly endless supply of stories seems one of the basic attributes of the Southern Indiana "master teller." Robert Adams, speaking of the Morgan County teller Thomas Sullivan says, "Sullivan conceives of himself as having, or more correctly, as having had before he began to feel the effects of old age, a nearly inexhaustible supply of "big ol' cock and bull stories." (p. 15) Says Sullivan, "Oh I could tell ya a million of 'em. Just sit down there if ya wantta hear some stories. I'll knock yer ears off ya." Robert J. Adams, "Raconteur and Repertoire: A Study of a Southern Indiana Storyteller and His Material," Master's thesis, Indiana University, July 1966.

6. The aesthetic of fitting a story to a specific situation is discussed by Richard Tallman in his notes on Nova Scotia teller Bob Coffil. Tallman

tells us that "Aesthetic appreciation is direction toward a story fitting a situation...the two [a story and its situation] are usually inseparable." (p. 126) Tallman notes that when Coffil tells stories he has learned from others he usually includes the context of their original telling. Likewise men at the community store, when asked about Coffil's stories, would usually describe a storytelling *event* rather than just tell the story. When asked if he had any favorite stories, Coffil thought not. "It's just under the circumstances, somebody's mentioned something that one of them'll come to me." Richard S. Tallman, "You Can Almost Picture It: The Aesthetic of a Nova Scotia Storyteller," *Folklore Forum*, 197, pp. 121-130.

7. Not all master tellers are as modest as Spiv. Kay Cothran says of her master narrators. "His fantastic wit needs, indeed thrives, on the praise of other men. More than a good, sociable self, he needs a character, a fantasy world built of style, and language is the technique he uses to create these," (p. 342) Kay L. Cothran, "Talking Trash in the Okefenokee Swamp Rim," *Journal of American Folklore* 87, no. 346, (Oct-Dec. 1974): 340-356.

8. 7/12/85. Gerald Helt, at Pert Helt's home. Interview with Margaret MacDonald.

9. 7/4/85. Gordon Helt to Margaret MacDonald.

10. Ibid.

11. 7/4/85. Gordon Helt to Margaret MacDonald.

12. Richard Mercer Dorson in "Oral Styles of American Folk Narrators" in Richard Mercer Dorson, *Folklore: Selected Essays.* Indiana University Press, (1972): 99-145.

13. 1/1/84. Gordon Helt at his home. To Margaret MacDonald. On being asked "Who taught you how to tell your stories so good?"

14. Robert J. Adams in his study "The Social Identity of the Japanese Storyteller" cites as one of the "Technical requirements for the development of a social identity as a storyteller" the "opportunity to practice storytelling technique in reinforcing situations." The importance of access to a reinforcing audience is stressed in his discussion of teller Tsune Watanabe. Robert J. Adams, "The Social Identity of a Japanese Storyteller," (Ph.D. diss., Indiana University, 1972).

15. Speaking of storytelling in the Okefenokee Swamp rim, Kay Cothran says "A great many men in the rim can talk trash when the occasion for it arises; properly sociable men are expected to be able to do so. Many enliven trash conversation with a clever experience story.

Thus competence in talking trash goes hand in hand with the essentials of male sociability. The Master narrator, however, goes beyond the basic essentials; he is a linguistic craftsman who works at his endeavor." (p. 342). Kay L. Cothran, "Talking Trash in the Okefenokee Swamp Rim, Georgia" *Journal of American Folklore* 87, no. 346, (Oct-Dec. 1974): 340-356.

CHAPTER 14
PASSING ON THE STORYTELLING
TRADITION

When I asked Spiv who he learned storytelling from, he was at a loss. He said that his father was a fairly taciturn man, not a good storyteller. None of his uncles stood out as particularly good tellers. Although I wasn't able to identify any influential tellers from his early years, Spiv did have a lot to say about one of the favorite tellers from his middle years. Clark Fitzpatrick, whose son married Spiv's niece, stands out in his mind as one remarkable storyteller. "That old Fitz could really tell them."

Spiv: I used to listen to old Clark Fitzpatrick.(1)
He used to be the best storyteller around this country.
He'd tell a new one ever time he seen ye.

"Awww," he said,
"I always knock at the front door and run at the back door with the axe..."
He said "I've never missed a man yet."
Spiv laughs.

Spiv, Jack McConnell, and other Scipio tellers still retell some of Clark Fitzpatrick's best stories. And they have a good stock of stories to tell on Old Fitz too.

Storytelling at the store seems to have been one learning spot for Spiv and many other Scipio tellers. Those who lived right in town got more exposure to this as children than Spiv, who didn't get up to Scipio until his teen years.

Esther: Edgar [her brother] used to when he was a kid...(2)
Spiv: In town...
Esther: ...Go over and sit on the store porch and listen to John Andy Day tell stories.
Margaret: He could tell stories?
Spiv: Yeaah...Ohhh...He could tell...
You couldn't tell when he was lyin'...
And when he was tellin' the truth...though.
Esther: But he could tell STORIES.
Spiv: But he was a good story teller.

Margaret: Edgar'd go over there and listen to 'em.
Esther: And he'd come home and be tellin' them...
And some of them didn't altogether suit Mom, of course.
She'd just as soon...he didn't go over there and sit and listen to this.
Spiv: Yeah. (chuckles)
That don't hurt a kid too much.
He'll do about what he's gonna do anyhow.

Jack McConnell had the same problem at his Dad's store. Jack lived right across the street from the store and must have spent much of his young life there.

Ledell: He listened to the oldtimers in the store talk.(3)
Jack: I had a lot of good storytellers...
Ledell: And he got his bad words...at the store...
His mother would wash his mouth out with soap...
And then the guys over there would put him up to sayin' it...these bad...
Jack: They'd give me a penny. To say a cuss word.
Ledell: And he was just cussin' up a storm...,I guess.
Margaret: I bet your mom loved THAT.
Ledell: Yeah. And they were payin' him to DO it.

Jack goes on to name some of the storytellers he used to listen to over at the store...Duc Hoppus, Fred Hoppus, Toot Greathouse, Clark Fitzpatrick (Old Fitz)...there seems to be quite a list.

I keep wondering if there are young folks in the Scipio community who follow in the footsteps of Spiv and Jack as storytellers. It is hard to tell. Evidence shows us that younger family members in a master teller's family may keep their own talents to themselves until the demise of the master teller, then move swiftly into a position of skilled teller.(4)

Spiv's younger brother Pert usually defers to Spiv when it comes to storytelling. Spiv is acknowledged as the master storyteller in the family though in reality, as Esther says of Pert, "He ain't far behind." Pert has developed his own repertoire which differs from Spiv's. Pert has a stock of standard jokes and throws one into the conversation from time to time. Spiv almost never uses this kind of jokelore in the storytelling settings at which I am present, relying entirely on humorous anecdotes which actually happened around Scipio.

Spiv's serious hearing loss and the quieter stance of his old age have removed him somewhat from the community storytelling arena. Jack McConnell seems willing to fill the gap, as we saw in his New Year's Eve performances.

As for the very young, it is usual for them to assume a listening posture in the presence of the old timers.(5)

I asked Jack McConnell if he thought hearin' Spiv tell all these years affected his telling style.

Jack: That's PROBABLY where I GOT it.(6)
Oh I've heard a lot of STORIES.
Ledell chimes in with a comment about Wally's twenty-
**   year old son:**
That old Scott Hines, he would rather sit...and watch
Wally and Jack and Spiv talk...than...ANYTHING.
Margaret: Is that so?
Ledell: Oh he LOVES to listen to them get into those
**   stories back there.**
So he just...he won't miss a meeting if he can help it...
Because he likes to hear them...go into their stories.

I ask if Scott tells stories too.

Jack: No, he just listens.
He's just right there.
Ledell explains: He just graduated a year or two ago.
He likes to listen.
Jack: He likes to listen.
He'll sit right there...you know back when he'd have
**   these...these New Year's Eve things?...**

He'd stay right there...
And just a teenager, you know...
He'd stay right there
And listen to a bunch of old fogies tell them things...
And really...really get a kick out of it.

I didn't get to know the young folks of Scipio well enough to collect them in story. Though I suspect that several can tell them, given the right environment. We know that Jack, twenty years Spiv's junior, is following in his footsteps, and certainly this author, twenty years Jack's junior, has absorbed a Jennings County storytelling style. Though I live in Seattle and speak both the casual non-dialect of that area and the formal academese of the university, when I return to Scipio I fall happily back into my native tongue. A brief episode from a 1983 conversation with Spiv and Esther reveals just how closely my own style is patterned on that of Spiv's tradition. Years of childhood listening have ingrained this style.

I'd been talking about an Arbuckle family bible that I bought at a farm sale years ago. I start talking about auctioneers and suddenly launch into story.

Margaret: Patsy and I used to go to sales.(7)
We'd get in the car an go rousting about the countryside, you know...
Go to SALES.

First sale I went to
I bought SEVEN TIN BUCKETS.
Seven buckets...
For a dollar.
SEVEN BUCKETS FOR A DOLLAR.

He held 'em up...
"Seven buckets for a dollar!
Where can you get a deal like this?"
I thought, "OH we NEVER have enough buckets at
    home...
My mom's gonna be so tickled to death..."
"I'll BUY 'em!"
Gave him my dollar, you know.
Took 'em home.
(in lowered voice) And ever one of them had a hole on
    the bottom.
Esther: Oohhh noooo...Good night!
Margaret: Ever single one of them had the bottom
rotted out.
Esther: Why they would put up somethin' like that...?
Margaret: Oh just so there'd be somebody like me
that'd BUY 'em.
    (laughs)
Spiv: (chuckling) How lucky could you BE?
Margaret: So I learned
    About goin' to sales.

In this brief episode are all the marks of the Scipio
storytelling. The clear formatted introduction "First sale I
went to...", repetition, truncated sentences for parallel
effect, use of quoted conversation, revelation of the
character's thought processes, varied voice...raised as the
auctioneer calls, lowered as I reveal the ruse, and the
playing out of the tale's ending through audience interplay,
with a final cap "So I learned about goin' to sales."

All of this stylizing emerges automatically, without
premeditation or previous telling of the episode. the

patterns of telling are internalized through a lifetime of listening, the Scipio teller is in effect "home-grown."

NOTES

CHAPTER 14

1.   1/1/84. Gordon Helt at his home. To Margaret MacDonald.
2.   1/1/84. Gordon and Esther Helt at their home. To Margaret MacDonald. Discussing Edgar Green.
3.   7/3/85. Jack McConnell and his wife Ledell McConnell at Gordon Helt's home. To Margaret MacDonald, Gordon and Esther Helt.
4.   The eclipse of storytellers by their older brothers or elders seems usual. Richard Tallman's informant Bob Coffil was eclipsed by his older brother during the brother's lifetime. Bob's son reports: "He [the older brother, Jack] was always telling stories, everywhere we went. The old man [Bob] was always quiet. He never talked so much.
And everywhere we went in the boat, Jack would tell the stories. He held the throne and people came to hear him talk. Everywhere we went, they knew him. The old man [Bob] never had much chance to tell stories when Jack was around, but he was kinda quiet anyway." (pp. 128-129) Eleven years after Jack's death, however, Richard Tallman selected Bob as "the best storyteller of the twenty to thirty men who regularly or occasionally spend their evenings in a small general store in the Blomidon community." (p. 123) Richard S. Tallman, "You Can Almost Picture It: The Aesthetic of a Nova Scotia Storyteller." *Folklore_Forum*, 197, pp. 121-130.
      Barre Toelken's storyteller Yellowman did not shine as a storyteller until after he moved from the shadow of his father-in-law, Little Wagon. Once Yellowman had moved out of the aegis of his father-in-law, Toelken "found him now an apparently inexhaustible source of tales, legends, astronomy, and string figures, narrating almost nightly to his family with a finesse I have not encountered in any other informant." (pp. 213-214) J. Barre Toelken. "The 'Pretty Language' of Yellowman: Genre, Mode and Texture in Navajo Coyote Narratives," *Genre* 2 (1969) pp. 211-235.
      It is interesting that these 'shadowed' tellers seem to have acquired through the years of listening with only occasional practice, the skills which enable them to move quickly into a position as 'master teller' once their family's master teller has vacated the chair. Robert J. Adams

in his "Social Identity of a Japanese Storyteller" stresses the acquisition of the "social identity" of a storyteller. Bob Coffil, Yellowman, and Spiv's brother Pert seem to have all of the required skills of the master teller in hand and lack only the "social identity" to move into the limelight. Robert J. Adams, "Social Identity of a Japanese Storyteller," Ph.D. 1972, Indiana University.

5.   In Richard Bauman's article on "The La Have Island General Store," he notes that "the younger men did not say much, but listened with interest to the 'old fellers that knowed everything.'" "By his early teens, a boy might be suffered to listen to the conversation from on the fringes of the group, but it was not until he reached the age of seventeen or eighteen that he would be allowed to speak, though only infrequently would he think of doing so. From the early twenties, eligibility for active participation increased roughly with age and worldly experience." (p. 333) Bauman, Richard. "The La Have Island General Store: Sociability and Verbal Art in a Nova Scotia Community" *Journal of American Folklore* 85, No. 338 (Oct-Dec. 1972): 330-343.

6.   7/3/85. Jack McConnell and wife Ledell to Margaret MacDonald, Esther and Gordon Helt, at the Helt's home.

7.   12/30/83. Margaret MacDonald to Esther and Gordon Helt at their home.

APPENDIX:
THE METHODOLOGY

How was this material collected?

With a variety of inexpensive cassette recorders. All had built-in microphones and were placed on the floor or on a table near the speaker but out of sight line.(1)

The first tapes were made in July of 1978, the last in October 1985. I visited Scipio regularly during the interim, usually about twice a year, as library conferences paid my way to the east coast and a short stopover in Indiana was not too expensive. My visits averaged about ten days each. The visits were intensive. I was usually taping from 9 a.m. to 10 p.m. every day while in Scipio. I ended up with over 200 hours of tape. One hundred hours have been selected for transcription.

How was this material transcribed?

I transcribed all tapes myself. Not that I had any choice, but I agree with Dennis Tedlock that "Far from being a mere clerical task, that act of transcription is ITSELF of analytical value when it is pursued with attention to oral qualities."(2)

I considered transcription systems developed by Dennis Tedlock, Elizabeth Fine, Virginia Hymes, and others.(3) Since I am asking the reader to consume many pages of transcript, I simplified my approach to the bare minimum. Caps indicate stress, other voice changes are given as stage directions. A break in line was made whenever the speaker paused. Dots were used for a more lengthy pause. Three dashes indicate a slight omission from the transcript, perhaps a listener response or a verbalization which seemed to clutter the printed text. Since my aim is to show the use of language *in context*, such omissions are rare.

Five dashes indicate a longer break from the transcript. Sometimes a teller would wander on to another topic and return to his original theme later. In developing the manuscript into a readable book, it was sometimes best to print thematic material together. I have not tampered with the *order* in which the statements were made.

How was this material elicited?

Most of the material used in this book occurred naturally in conversations. I had the tape recorder on during most of my visiting hours in Scipio. Some of the time was spent in asking questions about Scipio's history. But much was just visiting, eating meals, going on drives in the country, and stopping to see friends.

Since it was understood that I was interested in Scipio history and in Spiv's stories, people often brought the conversation around to local history, and Spiv was encouraged to tell his stories. Sometimes folks would prompt me to ask for a certain story. Other than that, the only thing approaching "interviewing" that occurred was my questioning of Spiv, Jack, my father and others about their attitudes toward storytelling.

I tried to play the role of my normal "self" when visiting.(4) I think I was perceived as a friend of the family, not an academic interviewer. Folks soon became used to the fact that a tape recorder was turned on anywhere I went. Spiv and Esther just kind of forgot about it after a while. This kind of "participant observation" was even carried to the extreme of "non-participant observation" during the 1985 New Year's Eve Party. I couldn't be there so I asked Esther, Jack, and Wally to set up a tape recorder and mail me the party.

Cases can be made both for and against interpretation of a culture by a *member* of that culture.(5) The folklorist as culture-member is in a position to ask himself myriad questions and to expect the thoughtful, to-the-point answer of one who knows just what it is that the folklorist needs to find out. Certainly a more cooperative, available, or insightful informant would be hard to find, allowing that the folklorist takes into consideration one major flaw...this informant is likely to tell the folklorist only what he *wants* to hear.

NOTES:
APPENDIX

1. *Oral History: From Tape to Type* by Cullom Davis, Kathryn Back, and Kay Maclean (Chicago: American Library Association, 1977) and *The Tape-Recorded Interview: A Manual for Field Workers in Folklore and Oral History* by Edward D. Ives (Knoxville: University of Tennessee Press, 1974) were useful in the early stages of my research.

2. (p. 123) Dennis Tedlock, "Learning to Listen: Oral History and Poetry" in *Envelopes of Sound*, edited by Ronald J. Grele, 1975, (106-125).

3. My transcriptions which began in 1980 were based mainly on the work of Dennis Tedlock, *Finding the Center: Narrative Poetry of the Zuni Indians,* (Lincoln and London: University of Nebraska Press, 1972). Others attempting ethnopoetic transcriptions in the journal *Alcheringa Ethnopoetics* (Boston University, 1970-1980) were also suggestive, as were recent works such as Peter Seitel's *See So That We May See: Performances and Interpretations of Traditional Tales From Tanzania* (Bloomington and London: Indiana University Press, 1980) and *Symposium of the Whole: A Range of Discourse Toward an Ethnopoetics*, edited by Jerome Rothenberg and Diane Rothenberg (Berkeley: University of California Press, 1983). *The Folktale Text* by Elizabeth Fine (Bloomington: Indiana University Press, 1984) gave an excellent summary of past attempts at transcribing oral texts, and offered intelligent discussion of the problems we have not yet solved.

4. I was strongly influenced early in the formation of this project by John Lofland's *Analyzing Social Settings: A Guide to Qualitative Observations and Analysis.* (Belmont, California: Wadsworth Publishing Company, 1971).

5. Lee Haring suggests that the folklorist turn his lens on himself, as an informant most likely to provide analytical comment on his own behavior. "Performing for the Interviewer: A Study of the Structure of Context" *Southern Folklore Quarterly* 36,(1972): 383-398.

INDEX

---A---

--B--

--C--